A Prayerwalk through Washington, D.C.

The Intercessor's Journal

Margaret Hadley
Illustrations by Millie Kuehnast

ISBN: 9798687747516

All Bible translations are acknowledged in text with the following abbreviations. Scripture quotations marked (**BSB**) are taken from the Berean Study Bible (The Holy Bible, Berean Study Bible, BSB) Copyright © 2016 by Bible Hub. Used by permission. All Rights Reserved Worldwide. Scripture quotations marked (**CSB**) are taken from the Christian Standard Bible®, copyright © 2017 by Holman Bible Publishers. Used by permission. Christian Standard Bible®, and CSB® are federally registered trademarks of Holman Bible Publishers. Scripture quotations marked (**ESV**) are taken from the ESV® Bible (The Holy Bible, English Standard Version®), copyright © 2001 by Crossway, a publishing ministry of Good News Publishers. Used by permission. All rights reserved. Scripture quotations marked (**GNT**) are taken from the Good News Translation – Second Edition © 1992 by American Bible Society. Used by permission. Scripture quotations marked (**HCSB**) are taken from the Holman Christian Standard Bible®, Used by permission HCSB ©1999, 2000, 2002, 2003, 2009 Holman Bible Publishers. Holman Christian Standard Bible®, Holman CSB®, and HCSB® are federally registered trademarks of Holman Bible Publishers. Scripture quotations marked (**KJV**) are taken from The Authorized (King James) Version. Rights in the Authorized Version in the United Kingdom are vested in the Crown. Reproduced by permission of the Crown's patentee, Cambridge University Press. Scripture quotations marked (**MSG**) are taken from The Message. Copyright © 1993, 1994, 1995, 1996, 2000, 2001, 2002. Used by permission of NavPress Publishing Group. Scripture quotations marked (**NASB**) are taken from the New American Standard Bible®, Copyright © 1960, 1962, 1963, 1968, 1971, 1972, 1973, 1975, 1977, 1995 by The Lockman Foundation. Used by permission. Scripture quotations marked (**NIV**) are taken from the Holy Bible, New International Version®, NIV®. Copyright © 1973, 1978, 1984, 2011 by Biblica, Inc.™ Used by permission of Zondervan, www.zondervan.com. All rights reserved worldwide. The "NIV" and "New International Version" are trademarks registered in the United States Patent and Trademark Office by Biblica, Inc.™ Scripture quotations marked (**NKJV**) are taken from the New King James Version. Copyright © 1982 by Thomas Nelson, Inc. Used by permission. All Rights Reserved. Scripture quotations marked (**NLT**) are taken from the Holy Bible, New Living Translation, copyright © 1996, 2004, 2007, 2013, 2015 by Tyndale House Foundation. Used by permission of Tyndale House Publishers, Inc., Carol Stream, IL 60188. All rights reserved. Scripture quotations marked (**WEB**) are taken from the public domain World English Bible, available at https://worldenglish.bible.

All photographs were taken by the author.

Dedicated to
JMH, REH,
CEW, BHW,
JLK, WLK,
and everyone with faith
"to pray always and
not become discouraged"
(Lk. 18:1, HCSB).

Contents

Preface
Map
Map Legend
Introduction
Prayerwalking Sites from A to Z
Conclusion: A Look Back
Notes
Contributors
Index of Nearby Metro Stations
Index of Major Prayer Topics
Endnotes

Preface

The Psalmist David wrote: "**The eyes of the LORD are on the righteous, and His ears are open to their cry**" (Ps. 34:15, KJV). What a privilege to intercede before a listening God! This book welcomes Christians to begin or continue their dedicated, extensive prayers for the United States. It offers Scripture verses and prompts for a wide variety of sites around Washington, D.C. Each place is labeled on the accompanying map. A site's address and a nearby metro station appear with every individual entry. The digital version is selectively illustrated, and the printed book features space for adding notes as well as your own prayers. This itinerary exceeds what an intercessor might profitably cover in one day. Although it can help move prayerwalkers toward the goal to "**pray without ceasing**" (I Th. 5:17, NIV), be selective. Aim to engage with the material over time. I encourage you to focus on places and topics that interest you. Craft your own agenda for intercession, whether you are at home or walking among the District of Columbia's monuments. If using this resource on site, pray with your eyes open. Stay aware of your surroundings. Wherever you begin, take time to praise God for His sovereignty, thank Him for time in His presence, and confess any sins that might hinder your prayers. Talk to the Lord discreetly, no matter where you are, about what you see along the way. Please note, it's more sensitive to intercede in silence or a low conversational tone, unless you already have permission to stage a public event. If you have never lived or worked in D.C., consciously cultivate this prayerwalk's challenge to empathize with people in the community. Make your own specific goals to grow in understanding as you faithfully petition God on behalf of the city. Pray for others to enjoy whatever highest good you might seek for your own loved ones or yourself. I encourage you to craft prayers that ask for God's best and for whatever may please the Lord most.

Let's approach the opportunity to intercede with humility regarding our own opinions or preferences, choosing to become more aware of our personal limitations and blind spots. Since the Lord's thoughts and ways are infinitely higher than ours (Is. 55:9), I know I cannot understand all God has appointed and allowed in a particular season, especially when it comes to those living and working in D.C. Looking beyond appearances at any point in time, we can lean on the Lord's sovereignty. The Apostle Paul encouraged the Ephesians, writing: "**He makes everything work out according to His plan**" (Eph. 1:11, NLT). Let's persistently pray for D.C. and seek the Lord's purposes, while acknowledging our trust in Him. Lift up God's longest-term intentions for peaceful negotiation and dialogue, echoing the Patriarch Job: "**no plan of Yours can be thwarted**" (Job 42:2, HCSB). Join me in praying for more people to identify reasonable common ground and work productively with others, particularly in this city. If there have been instances when you may have blocked constructive cooperation in the past, ask God to show you. Petition the Lord to inspire and enable you to be a wise team player at home, in your extended family, at church, at work, and in your community. May we understand others' perspectives more clearly and blaze consistently viable pathways toward living well together.

Map

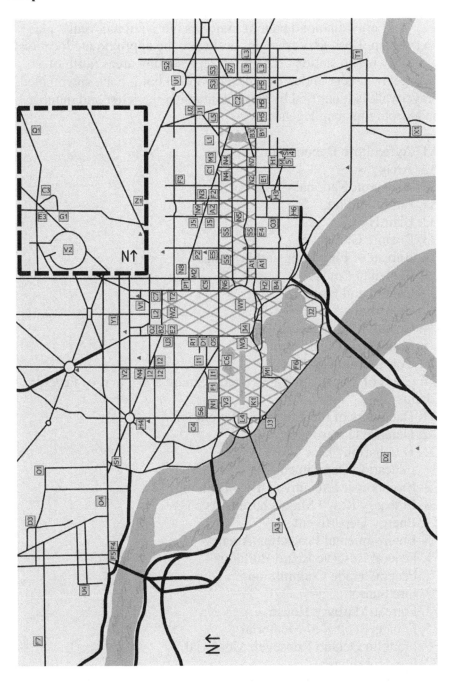

Map Legend

A gray diamond pattern indicates our National Mall's place on the map. Dark gray triangles designate the approximate locations of nearby metro stations. The inset, representing areas north of Georgetown, is bounded by a dashed line in bold. Each site on the prayerwalk is identified by a box containing the letter and number code from this map legend.

A1. Agriculture Department
A2. Archives
A3. Arlington National Cemetery
B1. Bartholdi Park
B2. Blair House
B3. Botanic Garden
B4. Bureau of Engraving and Printing
C1. Canadian Embassy
C2. Capitol and Grounds
C3. Cathedral
C4. Central Intelligence Agency
C5. Commerce Department
C6. Constitution Gardens
C7. Court of Appeals for the Federal Circuit and Court of Federal Claims
D1. Daughters of the American Revolution
D2. Defense Department
D3. Dumbarton Oaks
E1. Education Department
E2. Eisenhower Executive Office Building
E3. Embassy Row / Massachusetts Ave NW
E4. Energy Department
E5. Environmental Protection Agency
F1. Federal Reserve Board Building
F2. Federal Trade Commission
F3. Fire Station
F4. Forrest-Marbury House
F5. Francis Scott Key Memorial
F6. Franklin Delano Roosevelt Memorial
F7. French Embassy
G1. Greek Orthodox Cathedral

H1. Health and Human Services Department
H2. Holocaust Memorial Museum
H3. Homeland Security Department
H4. Hospital
H5. House of Representatives' Offices
H6. Housing and Urban Development Department
I1. Interior Department
I2. International Monetary Fund / World Bank
J1. Japanese American Memorial
J2. Jefferson Memorial
J3. John Ericsson Memorial
J4. John Paul Jones Memorial
J5. Justice Department / Federal Bureau of Investigation
K1. Korean War Veterans Memorial
L1. Labor Department
L2. Lafayette Square Park
L3. Libraries
L4. Lincoln Memorial
L5. Louisiana Avenue NW
M1. Martin Luther King, Jr., Memorial
M2. Mayor's Office
M3. Meade Memorial
M4. Mexican Embassy
M5. Museum of the Bible
N1. National Academies
N2. National Air and Space Museum
N3. National Council of Negro Women
N4. National Gallery of Art
N5. National Mall
N6. National Museum of African American History and Culture
N7. National Museum of the American Indian
N8. National Theatre
N9. Navy Memorial
O1. Oak Hill Cemetery
O2. Office of Management and Budget
O3. Office of Refugee Resettlement
O4. Old Stone House
O5. Organization of American States
P1. Pershing Park
P2. Post Office

Q1. Quaker School
R1. Red Cross
S1. Salvation Army
S2. Security and Exchange Commission
S3. Senate Offices
S4. Small Business Administration
S5. Smithsonian Institution
S6. State Department
S7. Supreme Court
T1. Transportation Department
T2. Treasury Department / Internal Revenue Service
U1. Union Station
U2. Unions
U3. U.S. Trade Representative
U4. University
V1. Veterans Affairs Department
V2. Vice President / Naval Observatory
V3. Vietnam Veterans Memorial
W1. Washington Monument
W2. White House
W3. World War II Memorial
X1. XFL D.C. Defenders
Y1. YMCA
Y2. YWCA
Z1. Zoo

Introduction

Before starting the second—and longest—section of my three-day prayerwalk through the United States' capital city last July, I noticed a worship service in a tent on the National Mall (see map: N5) near the Smithsonian museum (S5) where I once interned. Songs about trusting Jesus and looking forward to His future glory offered refreshing moments to focus on God first. Finding the way to Pennsylvania Avenue, I silently lifted up many institutions, organizations, businesses, and individuals while tracing America's Main Street north and westward to Georgetown.[1] Moderate temperatures in the 80s, falling as evening approached, boosted my energy to cover what might have been overwhelming during the District of Columbia's humid heatwaves. This break from typical late summer weather gave an abiding sense that the Lord was facilitating my prayer goals by doing what no one else could. The extended prayerwalk was a precious opportunity to seek new prompts for intercession and listen for the Holy Spirit's whispers in what others might call serendipity.

The highest-profile site on this part of the itinerary was the White House (W2), where I prayed for wisdom and God's will to be done as I navigated through an animated crowd. Fellow citizens vigorously advocated for both sides of pressing issues in front of the executive mansion. When I left the more touristy areas of the city, it became quiet. I asked God to fulfill every good purpose as He chooses and to multiply grace. Among many other requests for a wide variety of specific blessings on "**all who are in authority**" (I Tim. 2:2, NLT), I continuously searched for topics I simply had not prayed about yet. After years of regularly interceding for those in D.C., I have noticed sometimes the ways I pray for our government can become predictable. This itinerary was intended to help bypass getting stuck in plain repetition and avoiding requests mismatched with what is actually happening.

Deserved attention to the power centers clustered around our National Mall overshadows the area's colonial-era settlement, Georgetown. It predates the capital's urban center. I chose to spend a considerable amount of time prayerwalking in this distinctively quaint, historic section of D.C., because it vividly evokes layers of memory. Among the reduced scale of the buildings along M Street NW in Georgetown,[2] I was drawn to the Forrest-Marbury House at 3350 (F4).[3] I noticed this eighteenth-century gem just before my day's objective of reaching the Francis Scott Key Memorial at M and 34th Streets NW. Here, we remember the thick history surrounding our National Anthem (F5). A little tired from hours of walking while praying, I snapped a photo of the Forrest-Marbury historical landmark plaque. Seeing the façade's blue and yellow flag, I prayed for the leadership and people of Ukraine as well as their local harvesters. I also promised myself to learn more about that house's past.

Standing on what is currently Ukranian sovereign soil, the Forrest-Marbury House is mentioned in George Washington's diary on 29 March 1791, during his first term as president. After attempting to survey the area he envisioned for our new capital and hearing landowners' concerns, Washington wrote that he: "Dined at Colonel Forrest's to day [sic] with the Commissioners and others."[4] They finally reached an agreement on the District's boundaries and land divisions, signing official papers the following day. Their negotiations allowed the creation of our Federal City, a project designed to be self-funded by strategic land sales. One of the house's nineteenth-century owners, John Marbury, is best known for the Marbury v. Madison case establishing judicial review of legislation. This 1803 case enables courts to strike down laws judged to be unconstitutional, empowering the third branch of government to serve as a robust check on legislatures. When preservationists' concerns in the mid-twentieth century grew more urgent for appropriate conservation, the Forrest-Marbury House had been divided between residential apartments and a business.[5] Sensing the impact of major historical moments associated with this spot, I realized the prayerwalk route I outlined with partial understanding had led me to the place our capital began.

Creative compromise forged the United States' political capital along the Potomac River's banks. George Washington skillfully advocated for D.C.'s original ten square miles of land, drawn from Maryland and Virginia.[6] Its perceived neutral space for federal governance required a North-South bargain. Away from our first two Constitutional capitals located in free states, New York City and Philadelphia, this conciliatory move promoted a fledgling unity until individual equality and states' sovereignty could be more fully addressed. Whatever our personal views of this concession, it served larger purposes. Early cooperation by Northern and Southern states guarded the Revolution's success to establish and preserve the U.S.A. beyond England's War of 1812 attacks.

The history of our carefully crafted Federal City suggests many prayer topics for the present. Although this book's approach might appear novel, Biblical models inspired this practice of praying through history at a specific site. When King David publicly thanked God for safely bringing the Ark of the Covenant into Jerusalem, he sang of unbroken promises to the patriarchs: "**Remember His covenant forever, the word that He commanded, for a thousand generations**" (I Chron. 16:15. ESV). David praised God for protection: "**He allowed no one to oppress them; for their sake He rebuked kings**" (I Chron. 16:21, NIV). Israel's shepherd king punctuated this song with a refrain (I Chron. 16:34) that echoes through one of the several Psalms that incorporate repeated references to the past: "**Give thanks to the LORD, for He is good. His faithful love endures forever**" (Ps. 136:1, CSV). This Psalm is a prayer originally set to music that leads intercessor-worshippers through references to God creating everything and, much later, delivering Israel from slavery in Egypt so they could enjoy independence on their own land (Ps. 136:5-22). Reviewing a similar period of Israel's history, another Psalm evokes the freed slaves' jubilant experience: "**He brought forth His people with joy, His chosen with singing**" (Ps. 105:43, WEB). Another historically-rich Psalm suggests a higher purpose for chronicling events repeatedly: "**rise and tell their children so that they might put their confidence in God and not forget God's works, but keep His commands**" (Ps. 78:6-7, HCSB). May praying through our country's past and present solidify memory while building an unshakable hope in what God can do.

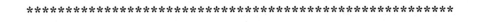

Prayerwalking Sites from A to Z

A1. **Agriculture Department**, 1400 Jefferson Dr between 12th and 14th Streets SW (Metro: Blue, Green, Orange, Yellow, and Silver lines, exit at L'Enfant Plaza or Smithsonian)

Along the National Mall, massive buildings house the Department of Agriculture. Ask the Lord to empower everyone who facilitates our country's consistently good food supply. The USDA building reminds us how important it is to maintain high standards while overseeing nationwide access to food. Lift up all the farmers and ranchers who enable our varied, vitamin-rich diets as well as the distributors and retailers who make foodstuffs accessible. Pray for the current Secretary of Agriculture, remembering universal concerns associated with health, family, stewardship, and vision. The Foreign Agricultural Service, occupying part of this complex, is dedicated to supervising related exports and increasing worldwide food security. Their ninety-eight outposts promote U.S. products and monitor agriculture in 177 countries.[7] Ask God to grant perpetual wisdom to individuals who, like Joseph in ancient Egypt (Gen. 41-47), have the power to help provide food during severe famines. Intercede for the multiplication of resources to feed people. May more places be blessed with harvests parallel to Joseph's extraordinary success: "**Joseph stored up grain in such abundance—like the sand of the sea—that he stopped measuring it because it was beyond measure**" (Gen. 41:49, HCSB). Petition on behalf of anyone you know battling food insecurity. Pray about one way God would want you to respond to others' practical needs for food. Promise Him you will take action on what the Holy Spirit prompts without unnecessary delays.

...ania Ave NW (Metro: Green and

...embrance as you pray about

...l Archives. Thank the Lord for all

...rces dedicated to preserving America's

...n for those who persevere to help augment

what ... **...ny shall run to and fro, and knowledge shall be increased**" (Dan. 12:4, KJV). Lift up each person employed or reading at the archives in the past year. May God give professional researchers the ability to find what they need for the arguments underpinning their next specialized lecture, course, or publication. Intercede that much of the research conducted here will shed light on our past in ways that help us understand how best to move forward. May the collections be preserved with excellence, yet always remain accessible for serious and significant research projects. Ask God to bless each person related to an author represented in our country's archives. Pray as the Holy Spirit leads for the distant relatives of our country's founders and past leaders, from those who have no knowledge of their connection to America's history to those who are keenly aware of their family's significant contributions.

A3. **Arlington National Cemetery**, 1 Memorial Ave, Arlington County, Fort Myer, VA (Metro: Blue line, exit at Arlington Cemetery)

From central D.C., Arlington Memorial Bridge leads straight to our national resting place. I encourage you to prayerwalk the cemetery in a respectful, silent manner. Noteworthy monuments include the Tomb of the Unknown Soldier and the eternal flame marking President John F. Kennedy's grave. That light was first ignited by Jacqueline Kennedy Onassis, who now lies beside our fourth president to be killed in office.[8] Thank God for our military's efforts to preserve the country and defend freedom. Thank Him for their families and descendants. Lift up everyone mourning at Arlington today. May the Lord comfort and heal them as they grieve. Intercede for a healthy approach to commemoration, asking that these soldiers' great sacrifices will never be forgotten or marginalized. Pray through a special benediction for those who remain faithful to God in the most challenging circumstances: **"Write, 'Blessed are the dead who die in the Lord from now on.' 'Yes,' says the Spirit, 'that they may rest from their labors; for their works follow with them'"** (Rev. 14:13, WEB).

B1. **Bartholdi Park**, 245 1st St SW (Metro: Blue, Orange, and Silver lines, exit at Capitol South)

Bartholdi Park's heart is the *Fountain of Light and Water*. Frederick Law Olmstead's design for D.C. parkland envisioned this work on the Botanic Garden grounds at the center of the National Mall.[9] Sculptor Frédéric Auguste Bartholdi, well known for his monumental *Statue of Liberty* in New York harbor, prepared this fountain for the 1876 Centennial Exhibition at Fairmount Park in Philadelphia. This water feature was among the earliest illuminated monuments in D.C., originally using gas lamps and being fitted with its first electrical lighting system in 1915. Although its location has changed multiple times, its celebration of water and light leads our minds back to the traditional quartet of elements: earth, air, water, and fire. Its cast iron was drawn from the earth and formed with fire. Its mechanisms propel water through the air to create a pleasing microclimate on hot summer days. We glimpse rainbow colors when sunlight hits it from just the right angle. Thank God for ordering His Creation, giving us the blessing of light (Gen. 1:3), and separating the waters (Gen. 1:6-7). Praise Him for keeping His promise to Noah, symbolized by the rainbow: "**I will never again destroy all living things**" (Gen. 8:21, NLT).

B2. **Blair House**, 1651 Pennsylvania Ave NW (Metro: Blue, Orange, and Silver lines, exit at Farragut West)

Blair House once belonged to a newsman among President Andrew Jackson's informal advisers. Encompassing a cluster of homes, it includes the house the Blairs built next door for their married daughter.[10] The site has been adapted to welcome our president's visitors. Pray for each person who has or will use the guesthouse this year. Intercede for the next guests' travel plans, remembering their needs for protection and strength. Ask God to give insight and timely ideas to each diplomat or VIP. May anyone with our president's ear be given words the Lord can use to usher in whatever change He would desire most. Think back to a time you received or offered hospitality. Reflect on your efforts and the Biblical guideline: "**Share with the saints in their needs; pursue hospitality**" (Rom. 12:13, ESV). Request the ability to be a good host or guest whenever opportunity arises.

B3. **Botanic Garden**, 100 Maryland Ave SW (Metro: Blue, Orange, and Silver lines, exit at Capitol South)

The United States Botanic Garden was moved in the 1930s from its axial nineteenth-century placement on the Mall between 1st and 3rd Streets NW and SW.[11] This garden idea, which our founders once contemplated, was developed through over 1,000 live plants and the nearly 650 different kinds of seeds supplied by Charles Wilkes's 1842 expedition to the South Seas.[12] Wilkes's domineering treatment of the crew and atrocities committed against people in Fiji necessitated court martial proceedings upon return.[13] Many of the ethnographical, animal, and geological specimens gathered during this circumnavigation of the globe enriched the Smithsonian Institution collection. The objects were first exhibited in the Patent Office Building, on the block from F to G Streets and 7th to 9th Streets NW, where the Smithsonian American Art Museum and National Portrait Gallery are now. First, confess that our government—unfortunately—backed an invasive and abusive expedition. May the Lord forgive us for this and help us learn from our mistakes. Pray Americans abroad will be thoroughly respectful now and in the future. Although the process of bringing plants and other scientific or educational materials to America was not always above reproach, the long histories of institutions utilizing these collections have benefitted the global community. Thank the Lord for orchestrating transformation beyond our hopes and expectations: **"We know that all things work together for the good of those who love God: those who are called according to His purpose"** (Rom. 8:28, HCSB). Lift up those who oversee this garden's facilities, including its branch across the river in Anacostia. Thank God for the scientific discoveries that have been made as a result of our botanical collection. When you can visit, I recommend looking for the rose garden outside as well as the orchid room inside. Pray for all who visit the garden today to experience wonder and appreciate the intricacy of the Creator's hand.

B4. **Bureau of Engraving and Printing**, 301 14th St SW (Metro: Blue, Orange, and Silver lines, exit at Smithsonian)

The Bureau of Engraving and Printing has produced currency and stamps since the Civil War.[14] Ask God to keep giving foresight and skill to the institution's designers, printers, and all other staff members. Lift up their efforts to thwart counterfeit money circulation. Reflect before the Lord on your attitude toward money and building wealth. Consider one of Jesus' teachings about this subject: **"Don't lay up treasures for yourselves on the earth, where moth and rust consume, and where thieves break through and steal; but lay up for yourselves treasures in heaven … for where your treasure is, there your heart will be also"** (Mt. 6:19-21, WEB). Remember something that once cost you a lot of money but now rests in a junkyard or landfill. Think through the kinds of opportunity and fulfillment that item provided as well as the reasons it is no longer yours. Confess any ways that financial considerations might have hindered your relationship with the Lord or others. Ask for supernatural strength to be a better steward of all the resources God has given you. Pray for grace to be more generous and consistently discerning as you give in the future.

C1. **Canadian Embassy**, 501 Pennsylvania Ave NW (Metro: Green and Yellow lines, exit at Archives)

Our neighbor to the north enjoys a prime location, in terms of diplomatic real estate, for the Embassy of Canada. Thank God for long-term, positive diplomatic relations between our countries. Growing up closer to Ontario than to any U.S. state, I remember how we crossed that international border without passports when I was young. Praise the Lord for the level of cooperation and trust this past openness exemplifies. Ask God to bless Canadian individuals and companies that supply our country with materials and services, as well as those who purchase U.S. goods. Pray that our steadily constructive historic relationship will continue for the substantial benefit of people on both sides of the border. Lift up the protection of waterways we share, such as the Great Lakes, Niagara Falls, and the Saint Lawrence River. Intercede for greater awareness of actual or potential harm to our common water supply. May those positioned to take action find viable solutions to any serious problems. Invite the Lord to sustain and empower the poor or marginalized in their country, particularly those who are losing hope. Pray for Christians in Canada and their fellowships as you feel led. May they enjoy **"righteousness, peace, and joy in the Holy Spirit"** (Rom. 14:17, WEB).

C2. **Capitol and Grounds**, from 1st St SE to 1st St NW and Constitution to Independence Avenues (Metro: Red line, exit at Union Station)

The Capitol Grounds were designed in 1875 by the same landscaper who envisioned Central Park in New York City: Frederick Law Olmstead. Near the western base of this naturally high terrain, the original inhabitants of the area—the Manahoacs and Monacans—held occasional tribal councils.[15] Bless these tribes' descendants as the Holy Spirit leads you. Thank the Lord that the tradition of gathering to make decisions here has been upheld from before recorded times. Petition that we will continue to honor this area's immemorial legacy of dialogue. Pray for the future of civil discourse and constructive compromise in this place. Walking through the park around the Capitol, you may notice plaques designating trees that represent different states or memorialize individuals' lives. Incorporate these names as prompts into your prayerwalk through this greenspace. If you do not have enough background knowledge to intercede with understanding in every case, you might offer the universal benediction from an Ascent Psalm: **"we bless you in the name of the LORD"** (Ps. 129:8, KJV).

Directly east from the Capitol building's central axis, note the Capitol Visitor Center that enhances the site's didactic role and ensures appropriate crowd control measures. This could be a good place to get out of the weather for a while or use the available facilities, especially if it's not too busy. Ask God to strengthen and guide those improving the experiences of many tourists and students who come to the Capitol each year. May their efforts help inspire visitors with an unforgettable experience of learning more about our Republic. Intercede for the security personnel who watch over our Capitol area night and day. Petition God to invigorate them when they feel weary. Pray that they will have all the alertness and skill they need to confront every challenge. Thank the Lord for those who are willing to serve in ways that promote the functioning of our representative government.

Congress gave Rev. Billy Graham permission to host a worship service on 3 February 1952 at the Capitol steps.[16] Thousands attended in the rain. Taking to heart Graham's call that day for prayer across America, Congress soon passed a bill, which President Harry Truman signed, to establish our National Day of Prayer. Graham was in town for an extended Washington, D.C., crusade from 13 January to 7 February 1952. He returned to hold services again in 1960 and 1986. Known for his straightforward presentation of the Gospel, Graham's preaching focused on repentance and life in Christ. One signature element of his large, revival meetings was the hymn "Just As I Am."[17] Pray that more hearts would open to its message of receiving saving grace through faith in Jesus: "waiting not to rid my soul of one dark blot.... I come!" Invite God to build up those who have recently understood the special joys of new life mentioned in this nineteenth-century hymn: "all I need, in Thee [I] find … welcome, pardon, cleanse … I believe." Rejoice over the lasting spiritual fruit from just one service on Capitol Hill.

Near the base of the Capitol steps, or wherever the given security situation and current events allow a good vantage point, pray about both houses of our legislative branch. The building's southeast cornerstone was set in the presence of George Washington on 18 September 1793.[18] Capitol facilities quickly became too small for the growing number of representatives, as more states joined the original union. It seems ironic that Jefferson Davis, an eventual separatist and Confederate leader, was the Mississippi senator who proposed a bill to enlarge this building in 1850.[19] Intercede about the relationships, priorities, and activities of senators and representatives. Pray for all our elected officials and the extensive staff supporting their work. Lift up those who seek the Lord's guidance in Scripture, echoing the Biblical song: "**Your Word is a lamp to my feet, and a light for my path**" (Ps. 119:105, WEB). May they enjoy abundant light to help us all move forward.

In preparation for this prayerwalk, you may have looked carefully into the legislature's agenda. Reflect on the bills you have heard about recently. Pray through all the ramifications of any potential or newly approved laws. Remember the country's budget and its obligations. Petition the Lord regarding particular concerns you have, based on your own, your family's, and your close associates' circumstances. If there is a recent law that has made an impact in your life or the lives of those closest to you, specifically mention it. Ask God for the strength and ability to function within our laws. Meditate before the Lord on Paul's exhortation: "**Let everyone be subject to the governing authorities, for there is no authority except that which God has established. The authorities that exist have been established by God**" (Rom. 13:1, NIV).

Since the prevailing philosophy of government's role has expanded considerably from our fledgling country's original, basic concerns for defense and leadership by the consent of the governed, consider all the areas of life impacted by our laws. Pray that our representatives in both houses will consistently exhibit wisdom and unselfish perspectives. Given their currently expansive role in regulating the concerns of daily life, ask the Lord to prompt elected leaders toward ongoing personal involvement in what have traditionally been called the works of mercy. May God open doors for our representatives to do significant community service by feeding the hungry, providing for clean water, distributing clothing, sheltering strangers, visiting the sick, freeing captives, and burying those who die without resources. Jesus' own teachings provide the foundation for these activities: **"For I was hungry and you gave Me something to eat; I was thirsty and you gave Me something to drink; I was a stranger and you took Me in; I was naked and you clothed Me; I was sick and you took care of Me; I was in prison and you visited Me"** (Mt. 25:35-36, HCSB). Intercede that substantive experiences helping people will deepen our representatives' compassion for others and broaden their awareness of suffering in America. Craft specific blessings for everyone in your church and community who does these works of mercy. Pray the Lord gives them more profound wells of respect, kindness, and generosity as they reach out. Ask God for excellent spiritual fruit to grow through regularly engaging in works of mercy, both in those who help and those who willingly receive. Petition for more grace to manifest spiritual works of mercy in your life: teaching, counseling, admonishing, bearing wrongs, forgiving, comforting, and praying.[20]

C3. **Cathedral**, 3101 Wisconsin Ave NW (Metro: Shady Grove—Glenmont Red line, exit at Woodley Park—Zoo; see map inset)

Pierre L'Enfant, the original urban planner for D.C., imagined this sanctuary to become "a great church for national purposes."[21] The Episcopalian cathedral's charter was not approved until roughly a century later (1893). If you wish, you might arrange a tour in advance to ascend the tower for a unique view of the church and the entire area. Thank God for collective prayer, memorial, and inauguration services held here to signify that many people in our country look to the Lord. Remembering their pulpit welcomed Dr. Martin Luther King Jr.'s final Sunday sermon in 1968, praise the Lord for using Christians to help with the ministries of peace and liberation. May we support this ongoing work, as Paul recognized that God has **"given to us the ministry of reconciliation"** (II Cor. 5:18, KJV). Pray that Jesus, through the Bible's words and the Holy Spirit's ministry, would draw to Himself every person who visits this place or hears one of its services. May God spiritually meet those who come here in a memorable way.

C4. **Central Intelligence Agency**, 2430 E St by 23rd St NW (Metro: Blue, Orange, and Silver lines, exit at Foggy Bottom)

Gathering information is essential for decision making that promotes prudent governance and diplomacy. As the Proverb says, **"It is the glory of God to conceal a thing: but the honor of kings is to search out a matter"** (Pr. 25:2, KJV). The CIA is associated with America's worldwide intelligence work. During the mid-twentieth century, recommendations were made for the CIA to appoint a coordinator for all our intelligence efforts, but this idea did not gain sufficient support until after the 9/11 attacks.[22] That multi-faceted, terrorist operation on our own soil underscored how refusing to share information might allow enemies to go unnoticed and unchecked. In 2005, a Cabinet-level Director of National Intelligence was appointed by President George W. Bush to help us avoid the pitfalls of poor coordination. Intercede for the leadership of our allied intelligence agencies, their staff, consultants, interns, and associates. Ask God to protect our officials while giving them the boldness, attention to detail, and perseverance necessary for their roles. Pray they will notice what no one else sees and make connections that lead to impactful discoveries. May they judiciously overlook what will result in wild goose chases or otherwise fruitless drains on time, energy, and resources.

C5. **Commerce Department**, 1401 Constitution Ave at 15th St NW (Metro: Blue, Orange, and Silver lines, exit at Federal Triangle)

The Commerce Department is dedicated to helping the American economy grow and creating conditions that lead to more opportunities for expansion. They conduct research, provide data, and set standards aimed at promoting fair, reciprocal trade among our states, territories, and over 86 countries.[23] Remember their leadership and initiatives. Lift up your home state's range of opportunities and all the entrepreneurs you know personally. Ask God to allow the economic growth of our country to spill over and bless many others. As Jabez petitioned: "**If only You would bless me, extend my border, let Your hand be with me, and keep me from harm, so that I will not cause any pain**" (I Chron. 4:10, HCSB). Pray for the economic well-being of the United States' inhabited island territories: American Samoa, Guam, Midway Atoll, Northern Mariana Islands, Puerto Rico, Palmyra Atoll, and the U.S. Virgin Islands.[24] May God give all our sole proprietors and job creators wisdom to handle aspects of doing business that may not be directly related to their product or service, such as compliance with codes and regulations, appropriate insurance coverage, real estate choices, renovations, investments, retirement planning, and sustainability concerns.

C6. **Constitution Gardens**, between the Mall's Reflecting Pool and Constitution Ave NW (Metro: Blue, Orange, and Silver lines, exit at Smithsonian or Farragut West)

The area containing a Bicentennial memorial, known as Constitution Gardens, used to be under water, but the Army Corps of Engineers began creating this parkland in the late nineteenth century.[25] Along the north side of the Constitution Gardens Pond, find a bridge to an island with a memorial honoring the 56 signers of the Declaration of Independence. After the Declaration's text asserted the country's new status as a free political state, it summarized the commitment each signer made: "with a firm reliance on the protection of divine Providence, we mutually pledge to each other our Lives, our Fortunes and our sacred Honor."[26] Thank God for the measure of faithful allegiance these founders showed our country. They remind me of the Prophet Jonah's promise in the belly of the great fish: **"I will pay that which I have vowed"** (Jon. 2:9, WEB). Reflect on any vows you have made in the past. Ask the Lord to help you fulfill every lawful obligation you have in ways that meet or exceed the horizon of expectation. Petition for mercy regarding times you have failed or waited to do what is right. Since some of the signers were slaveholders, pray against any lingering strongholds of darkness and moral blindness. Intercede for the proper perspective on others' limitations, struggles, and mistakes.

C7. **Court of Appeals for the Federal Circuit and Court of Federal Claims**, 717 Madison Pl NW (Metro: Blue, Orange, and Silver lines, exit at McPherson Square)

At the eastern edge of Lafayette Park, we find the U.S. Court of Federal Claims, handling all monetary lawsuits against the government, and the U.S. Court of Appeals for the Federal Circuit. The latter institution has a rotating Chief Justice spot, twelve active justices, and retired justices with senior status. It typically involves a life tenure that is subject to the standard of good behavior. Federal circuit appeals allow for judicial challenges based on particular subjects, such as patent cases, instead of being tied to a specific regional location. Petition God regarding every case considered this year, according to your knowledge of the docket. May their proceedings' outcomes exemplify wisdom and foresight. Lift up the individuals whose core interests are at stake. Remember people embroiled in long, expensive legal battles. Ask for the Lord's will to be done in the human administration of justice here. Pray that those who seek to uphold Biblical principles will have many reasons to rejoice over how our laws are interpreted. Intercede for God's eternal purposes to be served. As the Proverb says: "**Justice executed is a joy to the righteous, but a terror to the workers of iniquity**" (Pr. 21:15, BSB).

D1. Daughters of the American Revolution, 1776 D St at 17ᵗʰ St NW (Metro: Blue, Orange, and Silver lines, exit at Smithsonian or Farragut West)

The Daughters of the American Revolution began their historical and educational mandate through the initiative of women in the late nineteenth century. Its members trace their ancestry to patriots who fought and liberated America's thirteen original states from colonial oppression during the Revolutionary War. They support expert genealogical research and seek to "aid in securing for mankind all the blessings of liberty."[27] Praise the Lord for their families' legacy of promoting freedom. Ask God to empower the women of this organization to reach beyond their comfort zones to serve the needs of many more people. May they inspire others to follow an exhortation from the book of Hebrews: "**Do not neglect to do good and to share what you have, for such sacrifices are pleasing to God**" (Heb. 13:16, ESV). Reflect on a couple practical ways you plan to share in the next month. Pray for the follow-through to meet these goals.

D2. Defense Department, 100 S Washington Blvd, Arlington, VA (Metro: Blue or Yellow lines, exit at Pentagon)

Land for Arlington Cemetery and the Pentagon, southwest of the Potomac, includes part of the original diamond-shaped area George Washington chose for D.C. As headquarters of the Department of Defense, the Pentagon represents America's oldest agency and largest employer, overseeing the Army, Marines, Navy, Air Force, Space Force, Coast Guard, and the civilians who assist them.[28] Pray for each strategy session, operation, and review on their agendas this month. Lift up the current Defense Secretary, Joint Chiefs, every active member of the military, civilian support staff, and their families. Ask the Lord to fulfill His purposes through them. Echo one of the warrior King David's prayers over their lives: "**May the LORD, my rock, be praised, Who trains my hands for battle and my fingers for warfare. He is my faithful love and my fortress, my stronghold and my deliverer. He is my shield, and I take refuge in Him**" (Ps. 144:1-2, HCSB). May each one be well supplied and protected as they keep watch and fight for us.

D3. **Dumbarton Oaks**, 1703 32nd St NW, Georgetown (Metro: Blue, Orange, and Silver lines, exit at Foggy Bottom)

Georgetown's Dumbarton Oaks complex is overseen by our country's oldest college, now known as Harvard University. The museum boasts world-class exhibits of both Byzantine and Mesoamerican, or pre-Columbian, art. The ensemble includes a large garden and specialized research library. Perhaps you have already seen how their aesthetic expertise influenced Byzantine revival architecture at D.C.'s nearby Greek Orthodox cathedral, St. Sophia (G1, see map inset). Dumbarton Oaks, however, is also famous for the 1944 diplomatic talks that helped set the foundations for the United Nations.[29] Dumbarton Oaks' beautiful, serene setting facilitated the challenging discussions involved in persuading many countries to invest in the goals of internationally maintaining security and peace, fostering friendly diplomatic relationships, cooperating to solve global problems, and setting up the UN headquarters. Pray for those who encourage careful listening. Consider the Proverb: "**If you listen to advice and are willing to learn, one day you will be wise**" (Pr. 19:20, GNT). Thank God for peace and cooperation by thinking about the ways these diplomatic ideals have impacted a loved one's life or your own experience. May we come to embody such lofty goals more perfectly as we are transformed into His image. Praise Him for this place that has helped promote both aesthetic excellence and international rest.

E1. **Education Department**, 400 Maryland Ave SW (Metro: Blue, Orange, and Silver lines, exit at Federal Center SW or L'Enfant Plaza)

The Department of Education effectively centralized a number of existing offices in 1980. It aims to foster high educational quality and good student outcomes through research, awareness-raising, financial aid policy, and equalizing access.[30] Pray about the ways their efforts directly impact children and young adults all over the country. Ask God to guide the Education Secretary, department officials, school boards, administrators, and teachers. May our country's children be prepared and empowered to compete in the global marketplace. Intercede for American students to make uniquely positive contributions to society. If you know professionals setting education policy or influencing officials active in this sector, remember them specifically now. Lift up the schools in your community as you feel led. Pray for the intellectual, social, and character development of the school-age children you know. Petition the Lord to help them grow in ways that please Him, just like "**Jesus increased in wisdom and stature, and in favor with God and men**" (Lk. 2:52, WEB).

E2. **Eisenhower Executive Office Building**, 1650 Pennsylvania Ave NW (Metro: Blue, Orange, and Silver lines, exit at Farragut West)

Adjacent to the White House, the Eisenhower Executive Office Building is named for the longtime Army man, educated at West Point. Ike Eisenhower aided Generals Pershing and MacArthur, served as supreme commander in World War II, and became Columbia University's president before being elected to the country's highest office.[31] His legacy includes the interstate highway system that greatly expedites commerce and helps draw the country together in countless ways. His life evokes the kind of Renaissance person who can make contributions in a variety of areas. Similarly, Paul showed versatility in his ministry: "**I have become all things to all people, that by all means I might save some**" (I Cor. 9:22, ESV). Intercede for officials in our government who are being stretched to come up to speed quickly in ways that help us respond to current problems. Pray for all the ideas generated by executive branch staff that become policies influencing daily life throughout America and beyond. Ask the Lord to help the officials and support staff who serve our country as they promote executive initiatives that benefit Americans in the long term.

E3. **Embassy Row / Massachusetts Avenue NW** (Metro: Shady Grove—Glenmont Red line, exit at Woodley Park—Zoo; see map inset)

In the triangle between Wisconsin Ave, Garfield Street, and Massachusetts Ave NW—also known as Embassy Row—walk Bryce Park's perimeter or sit on a bench while praying for diplomatic efforts. Ask the Lord to give ambassadors every skill, opportunity, and resource they need to foster productive peace and beneficial cooperation among sovereign states throughout the world. May their efforts multiply blessings, as James wrote: "**Peacemakers who sow in peace reap a harvest of righteousness**" (Jas. 3:18, NIV). Pray our State Department maintains clear diplomatic vision to serve America's complex needs and best interests. Imagining the entire length of Embassy Row and diplomatic installations on nearby streets, intercede for many countries represented in our capital and stay attentive to the Holy Spirit's leading.

Remember adjacent areas that protect sovereign entities, like Switzerland's embassy between Cathedral Ave and Garfield Street NW. Independent states' outposts along Massachusetts Ave from Garfield Street to Rock Creek Parkway NW include: Nepal, Iraq, Cabo Verde, Azerbaijan, Vatican City, Finland, the United Kingdom, South Africa, New Zealand, Bolivia, Sri Lanka, Brazil, Denmark, and Italy. On or near Embassy Row from Rock Creek Parkway to Sheridan Circle NW, we find diplomatic installations of: Spain, Oman, Belize, Guyana, India, Turkey, Japan, Lesotho, Slovenia, South Korea, Marshall Islands, Chad, Côte d'Ivoire, Malawi, Cameroon, Myanmar, Costa Rica, Croatia, Madagascar, Kyrgyzstan, Haiti, Dominican Republic, Kenya, Armenia, Cyprus, Burkina Faso, and Latvia. South of Sheridan Circle and before Dupont Circle, on or around Massachusetts Ave NW, the neighborhood hosts diplomats from: Guatemala, Zambia, Bulgaria, Romania, Ireland, Greece, Paraguay, Sudan, Estonia, Morocco, Portugal, and Indonesia. Fewer than a dozen blocks north of the White House, between Dupont and Thomas Circles NW, note the embassies of Uzbekistan, Columbia, Trinidad and Tobago, El Salvador, Peru, the Philippines, Australia, Hungary, and Tunisia. Less than a year and a month after interceding on site for these areas of Embassy Row, I witnessed multiple direct answers to prayer for the growth of believers from the wide-ranging list of countries above. A world-wide baptism event was streamed for twenty minutes on 23 August 2020 by the church David Wilkerson started in New York City, Times Square Church. The celebration included videos with dozens of new Christians being baptized—at or near their homes—in England, Northern Ireland, Spain, Bulgaria, Trinidad and Tobago, the Philippines, and the U.S.A.[32]

This incomplete snapshot of Embassy Row, based on the area's occupants, is not intended to downplay any other diplomatic installations throughout the capital. As Paul wrote: "**I urge that supplications, prayers, intercessions, and thanksgivings be made for all people**" (I Tim. 2:1, ESV). Wisconsin Avenue, for example, hosts the Chinese and Russian embassies. Seek out any country's sovereign outpost that speaks to your heart. Consider structuring your intercession to cover associations of countries like the Group of Eight (G8) or NATO. Another option is the G20 forum, whose member states are responsible for about ninety percent of the world's productivity. Pray over multi-lateral negotiations and all the leaders involved, remembering their relationships, health, spiritual lives, and stewardship. Lift up believers and Christian fellowships in these places today, interceding for true peace and great joy in Jesus' perfect work of redemption. Petition the Lord to help each one multiply blessings in their local communities. Ask God to break through barriers that hinder the spread of the Good News, according to His sovereign purposes. May Christians around the world enjoy favor as they reach out and witness to their neighbors. Mention any believers you know personally in foreign countries now. Think of something you own or have used that was made in another country. Bless the people, and/or their surviving family and friends, who produced and transported that item. While you remember the above countries, invite the Lord to help the poor and marginalized who are facing drought or scarcity to identify more ways to innovate and thrive within their current challenges. Intercede for God to bless the forgotten in ways that bring Him glory and honor. Pray for breakthroughs that address the specific concerns of orphans, widows, the sick, and prisoners. May many believers and seekers receive God's best for their lives in this season.

E4. **Energy Department**, 1000 Independence Ave SW (Metro: Blue, Green, Orange, Yellow, and Silver lines, exit at L'Enfant Plaza or Smithsonian)

Our Department of Energy directly affects the daily lives of almost every American, because few of us are prepared and able to operate without the help of any grid. Lift up the current Energy Secretary, mentioning personal domains of wellbeing, relationships, and resource management. Invite God's wisdom to illuminate the plans and activities of everyone who works at this department now. Thank the Lord for our country's natural energy resources. Praise God for all forms of provision He has granted us, as the Psalm says: **"He has given the earth to all humanity"** (Ps. 115:16, NLT). Pray that we would continually improve our stewardship of America's energy sources. Think about the complex means of harvesting and delivering materials that fuel modern life. May we respect their dangerous qualities and exercise caution. Intercede for all those involved in the energy sector, remembering workers who harness solar, wind, natural gas, coal, and oil resources. Ask God to comfort anyone who might have suffered loss due to processes or accidents connected to the discovery and distribution of energy-rich raw materials. If you know anyone who has experienced this kind of harm, pray for that specific situation. Lift up the families and friends of those in the energy sector, covering all who benefit from this important commercial activity and who are perpetually concerned about its safety.

Remember the engineers and visionaries working to solve America's energy challenges. May God direct everyone making progress toward improved and sustainable battery power, especially those who focus on incorporating components that avoid serious environmental or social justice issues. Lift up individuals who have been exploited or risk being trafficked in cobalt mines that provide raw materials to make lithium-ion batteries for computers and electric vehicles.[33] Pray the Holy Spirit would inspire and guide ongoing innovation that could help us protect more people around the world from dangerous working conditions. Petition God to empower us to do a better job guarding the planet from avoidable damage. Reflect on your energy use before the Lord. How much electricity, natural gas, oil, and other energy sources have you personally used today? What energy have you shared with others, including stoplights, climatized buildings, mass transit, and artificially-lit interiors? Ask God to show you whenever you can conserve energy or however you might maximize a return on the energy sources you use. Intercede for increased wisdom and awareness surrounding energy consumption in our country. May we minimize waste and make "**the most of every opportunity**" (Eph. 5:16, NIV) and of each resource for God's glory.

E5. **Environmental Protection Agency**, 1200 Pennsylvania Ave by 12th St NW (Metro: Blue, Orange, and Silver lines, exit at Federal Triangle)

The executive branch has appointed this agency to help develop policy and oversee management of natural resources throughout the country. Since their efforts involve forethought, let's pray a Proverb over their work: "**you need guidance … and victory is won through many advisers**" (Pr. 24:6, NIV). Invite God to help them benefit from excellent advice and facilitate continuous, substantive improvement. Remember the agency's leadership, requesting the Lord blesses them with discernment. Pray about the air we breathe and the water our country uses every day, as you feel led. Lift up anyone you know who suffers from conditions that affect breathing or from airborne allergens, such as COPD or hay fever, according to their situations. May the EPA collaborate constructively with local governments, businesses, and landowners to protect our lakes and rivers. Intercede for the safe use of chemicals in governmental, commercial, and domestic settings. List any people you know who have lived through an environmental disaster, especially if they are still working to get back on solid footing. Reflect before the Lord on how current waste removal and treatment services, disposal, and recycling processes affect our air, water, and land. Petition God for greater wisdom and motivation to find innovations that improve upon best manufacturing and household safety practices. Ask God to give the EPA wisdom to facilitate optimal land management that will, for instance, help guard the quality of our plant- and animal-based food supply.

F1. **Federal Reserve Board Building**, 2051 Constitution Ave NW (Metro: Blue, Orange, and Silver lines, exit at Smithsonian or Farragut West)

The Board of Governors of the Federal Reserve System coordinates the country's central bank and its twelve regional branches. They aim to assure stability by overseeing prices, transactions, and interest rates as well as financial institutions.[34] As the Spirit leads, pray about the financial system in our country, the Fed Chair, the Fed's staff, and its consultants. If you know the location of your region's Federal Reserve Bank, petition according to God's best for everyone working at that branch now. For instance, D.C.'s area comes under Richmond's jurisdiction, but my home state of Michigan is divided into districts that answer to the Chicago and Minneapolis branches. If you have ever been expected to pay an interest rate over ten percent, lay before the Lord whatever led to that set of circumstances. Pray for more widespread freedom from economic dependence in our country. Intercede for those who are struggling to achieve financial independence, as Paul recommended: **"Make it your goal to live a quiet life, minding your own business and working with your hands…. Then people who are not believers will respect the way you live, and you will not need to depend on others"** (I Th. 4:11-12, NLT). Ask God to help us handle our resources wisely, uprooting any examples of imbalanced consumption patterns, inattention, and debt.

F2. **Federal Trade Commission**, 600 Pennsylvania Avenue NW
(Metro: Green and Yellow lines, exit at Archives)

The Federal Trade Commission is charged with protecting the country's consumers and encouraging competition through regulation and investigation.[35] If necessary, they assist law enforcement's role. Lift up those who fight for fairness in the marketplace. Petition for more widespread integrity, which pleases the Lord: **"False weights and unequal measures—the LORD detests double standards of every kind"** (Pr. 20:10, NLT). May God bless each of this commission's initiatives that help accomplish His purposes. If you know of anyone who has been the victim of commercial wrongdoing, pray about that situation. President Franklin D. Roosevelt was present for the building's cornerstone laying ceremony.[36] This facility represents large-scale governmental construction projects during the Great Depression. Thank God for the lives and legacies of people who had the chance to work and survive because this project was realized. Praise Him for preserving our country, especially our ancestors and neighbors' relatives, during the challenging Depression era.

F3. **Fire Station**, 500 F St NW at 6th St (Metro: Green and Yellow lines, exit at Archives)

Along 6th Street between E and F Streets NW stands the D.C. Fire Department Engine 2 station. Near the firehouse, or the first time you notice a fire hydrant on your prayerwalk, thank the Lord for the brave firefighters who face danger to serve this city. Praise Him for any time the efforts of these intrepid citizens mitigated, contained, and extinguished a blaze. Intercede for those who have suffered loss through fire, especially during the past year. Lift up everyone who has lost family members this way. Invite God to meet them and gently comfort them. Ask the Lord to empower the community to help people who have recently survived a fire. Intercede that they will demonstrate the Lord's generous heart without needless delay: "**He who supplies seed to the sower and bread for food will supply and multiply your seed for sowing and increase the harvest of your righteousness. You will be enriched in every way to be generous in every way, which through us will produce thanksgiving to God**" (II Cor. 9:10-11, ESV). May churches in the city rally around anyone facing this kind of struggle, offering hope and genuine friendship. If you know someone who has survived a fire, pray for the situation now.

F4. Forrest-Marbury House (see Introduction)

F5. Francis Scott Key Memorial, M and 34th Streets NW, Georgetown (Metro: Blue, Orange, and Silver lines, exit at Foggy Bottom)

This small park's Francis Scott Key Memorial is dedicated to contextualizing our national anthem and its author, who embodied the pernicious contradictions of the antebellum South.[37] "The Star-Spangled Banner" was first drafted on 14 September 1814 to celebrate an American victory in Baltimore. The actual Fort McHenry flag that Key saw flying at the end of the battle is now in the Smithsonian.[38] Each stanza of the anthem repeats its most famous line: "the land of the free and the home of the brave." Pray that we will more perfectly uphold the ideals of freedom and bravery than past generations. Ask God to show you ways to personify these noble aspirations. Popular versions of the song today do not usually include the fourth verse. This marginalized stanza speaks of citizens defending their homeland, a country blessed with "vict'ry and peace," whose motto remains: "In God is our trust."[39] The Psalmist expressed a similar resolve: "**Some trust in chariots, and some in horses, but we trust the name of Yahweh our God**" (Ps. 20:7, WEB). Intercede for at least two people you know whose confidence is in the Lord. May they understand their highest callings and depend on God for the strength to follow His purpose for their lives. Reflect on all the ways you may need to trust God more completely, and pray about these concerns as you keep walking.

F6. **Franklin Delano Roosevelt Memorial**, 1850 West Basin Dr SW (Metro: Blue, Orange, and Silver lines, exit at Smithsonian)

The Franklin Delano Roosevelt Memorial honors the only American president who was elected to four terms, leading the country through the Great Depression and most of World War II. He is also noteworthy for overcoming polio and learning to thrive while living with a disability. The articulated areas of this complex monument include waterfalls, quotations from each term, and a sculpture of FDR in a wheelchair. During his first inaugural address, he encouraged Americans who faced the Depression years: "The only thing we have to fear is fear itself."[40] Thank the Lord for giving us access to the Divine love that "**drives out fear…. The one who fears is not made perfect in love**" (I Jn. 4:18, NIV). Pray that Christians would completely embrace God's love. Ask the Lord to help us overcome fear in all its manifestations. Petition for an increase in testimonies that agree with this promise in Scripture: "**For God hath not given us the spirit of fear; but of power, and of love, and of a sound mind**" (II Tim. 1:7, KJV). Intercede for people who regularly face fear, such as those without basic necessities, individuals with serious health issues, those navigating problematic or violent close relationships, anyone in debt, and all who live paycheck to paycheck. May God show Americans pathways out of persistent fear today. This ensemble is the only presidential monument on the Mall that includes a First Lady's statue. Beyond being our country's longest active First Spouse, Eleanor Roosevelt crafted her own unique legacy—advocating for human rights and remaining politically engaged—in part by mastering communication opportunities in print, radio, and film. Pray for other women who are now supporting equality and civil rights in the public discourse.

F7. French Embassy, 4101 Reservoir Rd NW (Metro: Blue, Orange, and Silver lines, exit at Foggy Bottom)

Our country's oldest ally, France, maintains its embassy just north of Georgetown University. After French individuals had provided aid to our revolutionaries for years, their monarchy became the first to recognize America's independent status during the Revolutionary War. Our bilateral treaties expressing amity, commerce, and military alliance were signed on 6 February 1778 and ratified in May. Primary motivations for early cooperation included France's longstanding rivalry with England, their recent territorial losses in the French and Indian Wars (1763), and their desire to conquer the British West Indies.[41] The French Navy was instrumental in winning the crucial Battle of Yorktown (1781). During America's precarious early years, this support from a major European power made an enormous impact. In the best cases, close diplomatic friendships help preserve both parties. As the Proverb says: "**A man of many companions may be ruined, but there is a friend who sticks closer than a brother**" (Pr. 18:24, WEB). Through France's various regime changes, our diplomatic relationship has evolved over the centuries. Lift up the ongoing, significant connections between our countries, as the Holy Spirit leads.

G1. Greek Orthodox Cathedral, St. Sophia, 2815 36th St at Garfield St NW (Metro: Shady Grove—Glenmont Red line, exit at Woodley Park—Zoo; see map inset)

The revivalist design of this church, inside and out, was developed in consultation with respected iconographers and historical experts from nearby Dumbarton Oaks (D3).[42] Although the name seems to suggest there's a saint called Sophia, a good translation is 'Holy Wisdom.' Divine wisdom can be interpreted as referring to Jesus. Paul succinctly conveyed this idea: "**Christ the power of God and the wisdom of God**" (I Cor. 1:24, NIV). Pray for more perfect wisdom among believers in the diverse, worldwide body of Christ. Ask God to give you the discernment you need in your particular season of life. Thank the Lord for maintaining a witness of His wisdom and holy Word in the Greek world from antiquity to our own day.

H1. **Health and Human Services Department**, 330 C St at 3rd St SW (Metro: Blue, Orange, and Silver lines, exit at Federal Center SW)

Public health involves working to mitigate dangers to the wellbeing of the entire human family, including hygiene concerns associated with water purity, food protection, and air quality. Lift up all who work to help society thrive by supporting scientific advances that inform guidelines about protocols to diagnose illnesses, treatments for diseases, and vaccines.[43] Intercede for those making decisions that promote better health and vibrant longevity. Ask God to give wisdom to policy makers and scientists who work to tackle the problems associated with diseases and chronic health issues. These challenges affect every continent, as we have seen during the COVID-19 pandemic that even prompted quarantines in Antarctica. May the Lord guide leaders who can implement the most appropriate responses to these threats: "**Make the path of your feet level. Let all of your ways be established**" (Pr. 4:26, WEB). Pray for everyone you know facing public health risks, including anyone pregnant in America's Zika-infected regions, or people with asthma in smog-filled cities. Thank God for the measure of health He has given you now.

H2. **Holocaust Memorial Museum**, 100 Raoul Wallenberg Pl SW (Metro: Blue, Orange, and Silver lines, exit at Smithsonian)

The United States Holocaust Memorial Museum honors all who suffered and died under Nazi German oppression, surveys the racism and Fascism linked to these twentieth-century atrocities, and recognizes survivors' liberation associated with Allied victory in World War II. I encourage you to visit their exhibits virtually or in person, especially if you have never been through a major Holocaust museum. Thank the Lord that the worst times of persecution have not negated God's promise to the Patriarch Abraham, who has been called the "**father of all who believe**" (Rom. 4:16, NLT). Intercede for the Lord to keep on fulfilling His original covenant with Abraham and his Jewish descendants: "**I will bless you, I will make your name great, … and all the peoples on earth will be blessed through you**" (Gen. 12:2-3, HCSB). Pray for living Holocaust survivors and their families. May they multiply their best contributions to the world.

Elsewhere during your prayerwalk, you might pass by a synagogue. Silently and respectfully lift up this and other Jewish gatherings in the capital, as you keep walking along. Ask God to protect all the Jews who live in and visit this area, requesting special blessings that will encourage them as they seek the Lord. God told the Patriarch Abraham: "**through your offspring all nations of the earth will be blessed, because you have obeyed My voice**" (Gen. 22:18, BSB). Praise God for keeping repeated promises to Abraham that his descendants would be a blessing.

H3. **Homeland Security Department**, 300 7th St at D St SW (Metro: Blue, Green, Orange, Yellow, and Silver lines, exit at L'Enfant Plaza)

While considering the Department of Homeland Security, thank the Lord for the measure of safety we enjoy in this country. Praise Him for those who have identified and thwarted dangerous plots against us. Intercede for everyone who labors under the umbrella of national security. Ask God to help them do their jobs without violating the Bill of Rights' Fourth Amendment intended to protect us from "unreasonable searches and seizures."[44] May the saints live in such a way that extensive searches could not discover something problematic. Petition for more widespread integrity beyond reproach, as the Proverb encourages: "**The fear of the LORD is the beginning of knowledge; fools despise wisdom and discipline**" (Pr. 1:7, HCSB). If anything in your life might be considered unlawful or even questionable by Biblical or legal standards, begin the process of repentance. Invite the Holy Spirit to reveal the best possible way to make it right. Similarly, if any Americans are aware of someone engaging in criminal activity today or planning to harm others, pray about how they will sensibly handle their ethical and legal responsibilities regarding that knowledge.

H4. **Hospital**, 900 23rd St NW (Metro: Blue, Orange, and Silver lines, exit at Foggy Bottom)

Lift up patients, doctors, nurses, caregivers, and administrators at this university hospital and all other academic research hospitals in our country. Ask the Lord to use these institutions to improve effective and accessible healthcare. Pray for their staff in training to have unfailing energy, integrity, and superlative powers of observation. May God give alertness and excellent skill to anyone who might be sleep deprived or otherwise taxed while helping patients. Intercede for everyone who needs to be in the hospital today and those who have a loved one under constant medical care. If you know a person who is, recently was, or soon will be admitted to a hospital, mention that individual specifically. If you have ever benefitted from care in a teaching hospital, pray God blesses the people who helped you. Consider the times when you have cared for others' physical needs in some capacity. Meditate on those experiences and ask for discernment about future opportunities to facilitate healing. As Jesus said to His disciples: "**whatever you did for one of the least of these brothers and sisters of Mine, you did for Me**" (Mt. 25:40, CSB).

H5. House of Representatives' Offices, 1 and 27 Independence Ave SE and 45 Independence Ave SW (Metro: Red line, exit at Union Station or take Blue, Orange, and Silver lines to Capitol South)

South of the Capitol, walk around or past the trio of blocks with the Cannon, Longworth, and Rayburn House Office Buildings. Pray for renewed attention in our system to the high standards of Mosaic law. May the Lord empower legislators ready to defend the innate right to love God above all others, live free from idolatry, maintain pure language, observe the Sabbath, and honor parents (Ex. 20:3-12). Ask the Lord to weigh heavily on consciences whenever someone murders, commits adultery, steals, misrepresents facts, or covets (Deut. 5:17-21). Petition God to uproot disorder among us. Jesus warned His disciples about tumultuous times: "**Because lawlessness will multiply, the love of many will grow cold**" (Mt. 24:12, HCSB). Invite the Lord to increase our love and respect for other people. Name your own elected representative in the House as well as the Speaker, Majority Leader, Minority Leader, Whips, Committee Chairs, and any other members you feel led to lift up in prayer. Since congressional committees regulate internal processes and perform executive oversight, remember all the House of Representatives' committees, highlighting any future or ongoing hearings you know of right now. Intercede for their staff and anyone involved in drafting legislation or budget proposals, requesting that their relationships help support what is best for the country. Ask God to direct the work of lobbyists, who impact the legislative process in a variety of ways. If you can think of a particular advocacy block or lobbying group, take time to pray about them as you feel led.

H6. **Housing and Urban Development Department**, 451 7th St at D St SW (Metro: Blue, Green, Orange, Yellow, and Silver lines, exit at L'Enfant Plaza or Smithsonian)

The Department of Housing and Urban Development was empowered by the 1968 Civil Rights Act to fight housing discrimination, and it actively promotes affordable housing options.[45] Intercede for people living in project housing all over the country. Pray a blessing from Proverbs over each household: **"By wisdom a house is built, and by understanding it is established; by knowledge the rooms are filled with all precious and pleasant riches"** (Pr. 24:3-4, ESV). Ask the Lord to uproot problems that might undermine project neighborhoods by the power of His Spirit, bringing unprecedented transformation in ways that would please God the most. Lift up those who struggle with homelessness and encounter prejudice when looking for a place to live today. Petition they will find what they need. Thank the Lord for every unbiased landlord who is willing to welcome tenants from all backgrounds and age ranges. Pray God will help residents as they work on building up their communities. May the Lord keep using individuals He's positioned in specific areas to have a positive, long-term impact.

11. **Interior Department**, 1925 Constitution Ave and 1849 C St NW (Metro: Blue, Orange, and Silver lines, exit at Smithsonian or Farragut West)

Our Department of the Interior is sometimes called the department of "everything else," because it has covered a broad range of domestic affairs from D.C. infrastructure and oversight for universities to supervising the use of wildlife and public lands.[46] The Interior Department's reach even includes overseeing America's hospitals. Its department museum, located in the building on C Street, provides one way to learn more about its activities. Praise God for at least three specific ways in which our country's domestic issues are being well managed. Lift up the Secretary, staff, officials, consultants, and their families. May they do the tasks before them with wisdom and excellence, contributing to stability and domestic tranquility. Pray for the people who depend most upon the approval and completion of future Interior Department projects. A bit farther west, the Office of Surface Mining Reclamation and Enforcement is part of the Interior Department that deals with environmental concerns related to coal production.[47] Thank God that our government has made efforts to reclaim former mining areas and actively restore habitats to improve our environment. Praise the Lord for the ways that mining has increased knowledge and supported advances in technology. As it says in the book of Job: "**A miner puts an end to the darkness; he probes the deepest recesses for ore in the gloomy darkness. ... He cuts out channels in the rocks, and his eyes spot every treasure**" (Job 28:3 and 10, CSB). May we conserve and wisely employ our resources.

12. **International Monetary Fund / World Bank**, 1900
Pennsylvania Ave, 700 19th St, and 1818 H St NW (Metro: Blue,
Orange, and Silver lines, exit at Farragut West)
     The International Monetary Fund includes an overwhelming
majority of the world's countries, having significantly expanded
from its original incarnation after World War II. This organization
aims to improve global financial security, promoting growth among
both domestic and international economies.[48] It works to foster
cooperation in the hope of limiting economic hardship. Next door is
the World Bank, created at the same time as the IMF. This bank
prepares loans and provides counsel for countries—especially as
they seek to eradicate poverty and increase overall prosperity. Thank
God for any time an initiative of the IMF or World Bank has
succeeded in making people's lives better. Pray for officials at all
levels with the integrity to help guard the process of allowing acutely
needed resources to reach the poorest among us. Ask the Lord to
comfort and empower the disadvantaged who face overwhelming
situations. May God open their eyes to feasible opportunities. **"For
You have been a stronghold to the poor, a stronghold to the
needy in his distress, a refuge from the storm, a shade from the
heat"** (Is. 25:4, WEB). Intercede for the end of the most devastating
kinds of poverty, according to the Lord's timetable and sovereign
purposes.

J1. **Japanese American Memorial**, between D St, New Jersey Ave, and Louisiana Ave NW (Metro: Red line, exit at Union Station)

Across from Senate Park, look for the Japanese American Memorial on Louisiana Avenue. Dedicated in 2000, it reminds us of Japanese Americans who fought for our freedoms in World War II as well as the roughly 120,000 Japanese Americans who were imprisoned in camps during the war.[49] These falsely accused compatriots remind me of when the Prophet Jeremiah was incarcerated for nothing more than faithfully communicating what God told him to share with King Zedekiah: **"What crime have I committed against you or your attendants or this people, that you have put me in prison?"** (Jer. 37:18, NIV) Thank the Lord for this monument's formal and visible acknowledgment of the injustices Japanese-American citizens experienced. Praise Him for every example of honorable service and resilience among the Americans whose ancestors came from Japan. Pray that our country would never again target innocent citizens during wartime or seasons of uncertainty. Ask the Lord to continue healing the country's wounds. May God show us other significant ways to move toward reconciliation.

J2. Jefferson Memorial, 16 East Basin Dr SW (Metro: Blue, Orange, and Silver lines, exit at Smithsonian)

An impressive flight of stairs leading from the Tidal Basin's waterside path aggrandizes the open-air Jefferson Memorial. It is plainly the smallest building anchoring the Mall's axes that intersect at Washington's monument. The building's obvious architectural references to the Pantheon, a pagan sanctuary in Rome dedicated to ancient planetary gods, contrast with the monument's focus on a single man.[50] The importance of Roman republican government in inspiring our Constitution is reflected in its language of architectural form. Jefferson's leadership in drafting the Declaration of Independence, which we associate with the birth of America on 4 July 1776, helped pave the way toward representative governance in our country. His memorial includes excerpts from the Declaration. This landmark document confronted tyranny by articulating basic human rights that were partially addressed in his time. Jefferson wrote: "all men are created equal … endowed by their Creator with certain inalienable Rights … Life, Liberty and the pursuit of Happiness."[51] Thank God that the founders' ultimate goal was championing rights and fighting for freedoms. May the Lord help us embrace the equality that America's founding documents invite us to seek and enjoy. Pray for wisdom to pursue life, liberty, and happiness in ways that will please God. Remember people alive today whose human rights would not have been recognized in the Constitution's original form, such as women and contemporary descendants of slaves. Intercede that we will be encouraged by instances when our founding documents were updated and appreciate the progress we have made since 1776. If you personally know anyone lacking equality or freedom, name that person specifically now.

Other quotes on the walls come from Jefferson's writings that promote freedom of religion, encourage public education, and—albeit ironically—denounce slavery. The monument's interior frieze enshrines what he wrote in a letter (1800) to Benjamin Rush: "I have sworn upon the altar of God eternal hostility against every form of tyranny over the mind of man."[52] May we live up to this ideal by first exercising discipline within our own minds. Reflect on Paul's words: **"We destroy arguments and every lofty opinion raised against the knowledge of God, and take every thought captive to obey Christ"** (II Cor. 10:5, ESV). Petition for the ability to win mental battles. Ask God for personal victory in this area. Pray that you will not avoid or forget to champion any good ideas that the Lord gives you. Silently bless every person who approaches this memorial in the coming week. May visitors be inspired to cultivate an even higher level of mental self-control than they currently enjoy.

J3. **John Ericsson Memorial**, 2912 Independence Ave SW (Metro: Blue, Orange, and Silver lines, exit at Foggy Bottom)

South of the Lincoln Memorial we find a sculpted reminder, dedicated in 1926, that immigrants have an opportunity to realize their dreams in America. Pray for all the immigrants in America now. The Swedish-born immigrant, John Ericsson, transformed ship propulsion in the mid-nineteenth century by engineering the race-winning USS Princeton steamer of 1843.[53] From ancient times, sea travel had relied on rowers' labor whenever sails could not harness sufficient wind power. Man-powered ships are directly linked to problematic labor practices. Ezekiel cited Tyre's maritime system as relying on both sails and rowing: **"they took a cedar from Lebanon to make a mast for you. Of oaks of Bashan they made your oars"** (Ezek. 27:5-6, ESV). When Alexander the Great conquered Tyre, he either slaughtered or enslaved the entire island.[54] By contrast, Captain Ericsson's modern designs were part of the technological revolution that shifted non-sailing sea travel definitively away from rowing, which obviously required manual labor. The screw propeller he invented for the USS Monitor (1862) assured the Navy's blockade that effectively undermined the Confederacy. This mechanical breakthrough, therefore, helped preserve the Union during the Civil War. Thank God for the ways inventors have contributed directly to the ongoing fight for universal human freedom.

J4. **John Paul Jones Memorial**, 17th St and Independence Ave SW (Metro: Blue, Orange, and Silver lines, exit at Smithsonian)

Before America's independence was declared, John Paul Jones volunteered for service at sea in 1775. Although the Continental Navy initially relied on commandeered merchant vessels and rarely had optimal equipment to help win battles, Jones fearlessly brought the fight to the enemy. He crossed the Atlantic to attack Whitehaven on England's western coast.[55] Despite his failure to convince the newly independent colonies to maintain a navy after winning the Revolutionary War, he is considered one of our Navy's founding fathers. Praise God for the audacity to fight along the enemy's shoreline, regardless of England's enduring reputation as one of the world's foremost naval powers. May our Navy continue modeling boldness. Lift up America's troops today. May they be supported and fortified like King David: **"It is God Who arms me with strength and keeps my way secure. ... He trains my hands for battle"** (II Sam. 22:33 and 35, NIV). Thank the Lord for building up our naval forces and filling their ranks with volunteers. Ask God to accomplish His purposes through the Navy's ongoing work. Pray for the health—spiritual, mental, relational, physical—and safety of all Americans on the high seas.

J5. **Justice Department / Federal Bureau of Investigation**, 935 and 950 Pennsylvania Avenue NW (Metro: Blue, Orange, and Silver lines, exit at Federal Triangle)

Our Department of Justice and the Federal Bureau of Investigation stand on opposite sides of Pennsylvania Avenue. These institutions constantly work to build and pursue cases that help ensure our laws are respected. Invite God to guide the current Attorney General. Pray about the priorities and daily activities of this institutions' public servants. Ask the Lord to orchestrate outcomes that glorify Him: **"For the LORD loves justice, and does not forsake His saints; they are preserved forever"** (Ps. 37:28, NKJV). May justice be upheld according to the law. If you know people directly affected by the department's investigations or judicial rulings on their cases, lift up their specific situations. Petition that victims' rights will be championed and convicted perpetrators treated in ways that deter future crimes. Pray for those who have experienced wrongdoing, asking God to defend their cause. Thank the Lord that all wrongs will be addressed when His eternal justice is ultimately served. Remember individuals who live in ways that help preserve justice in this country. Reflect in prayer on how the Prophet Micah summarized our personal duties to uphold what is right: **"He has told you what is good and what it is the LORD requires of you: to act justly, to love faithfulness, and to walk humbly with your God"** (Mic. 6:8, HCSB).

K1. **Korean War Veterans Memorial**, on the Mall between Independence Ave SW and the Reflecting Pool (Metro: Blue, Orange, and Silver lines, exit at Foggy Bottom)

The Korean War Veterans Memorial is dedicated to the 5.8 million Americans who served and the 36,574 who were lost between 1950 and 1953.[56] Bless God for strengthening all who followed orders to help preserve the free areas of Korea. Lift up individuals who live with the results of this war every day, including the families of the more than 100,000 veterans who were wounded. Pray about conditions on the Korean peninsula today, as you feel led. The memorial's over-life-sized representations of soldiers, arranged in a triangle, lead the eye toward a pool where an inscribed wall reminds us that "Freedom is not free." Sacrifice is an essential part of a mature Christian's experience, training us as we seek to imitate our Lord Jesus. **"But when Christ had offered for all time a single sacrifice for sins, He sat down at the right hand of God…. For by a single offering He has perfected for all time those who are being sanctified"** (Heb. 10:12 and 14, ESV). Praise God for the efficacy of Jesus' death on the Cross and His resurrection. Thank the Lord for the good news that we can be forgiven and delivered due to His perfect work of salvation. Pray for every person close to you who has trusted in Jesus for true peace with God.

L1. **Labor Department**, 200 Constitution Ave NW (Metro: Green and Yellow lines, exit at Archives)

The Department of Labor's mandate is "to foster, promote and develop the welfare of working people, to improve their working conditions, and to enhance their opportunities for profitable employment."[57] Ask God to give the agency's officials—from its current Labor Secretary to the interns—greater vision, capability, and diligence to help America's workers. Pray for everyone in the country who is working this year, reflecting on the Proverb: "**There is profit in all hard work, but endless talk leads only to poverty**" (Pr. 14:23, HCSB). Intercede for the specific concerns of anyone you know who is underemployed or involuntarily out of a job. Lift up all the employed individuals in your extended family. Bless their employers and the educators who helped them qualify for their current positions. Thank God for the ways our country's workers provide, directly and indirectly, for Americans at both ends of the spectrum who are not of working age. May the Lord continue to empower our workers to bless others.

L2. **Lafayette Square Park / BLM Plaza**, from 15th to 17th Streets and Pennsylvania Ave to H St NW (Metro: Blue, Orange, and Silver lines, exit at McPherson Square)

Lafayette Square Park was named for the first foreign dignitary to visit the White House. General Gilbert du Motier, or the Marquis de Lafayette, honorably served the American Revolutionary cause. He helped draw our ally, France, into the war and fought under Washington's command. Lafayette was known for generosity, valor, and perseverance. The site, unfortunately, also brings to mind an era when society was openly dependent upon forced labor. Lafayette Park reminds us of an oppressive social order, because it was formerly used as a slave market.[58] Many, in the past, anticipated slavery to be part of society—so much so that the Ten Commandments mentioned it as something commonplace: "**You shall not covet your neighbor's … male servant, or his female servant, or his ox, or his donkey, or anything that is your neighbor's**" (Ex. 20:17, ESV). Ask God to free our minds and heal our country from the long-term wounds of allowing subjugation and enabling marginalization. Pray we never backslide. Ask God to give our country total victory over uprooting that twisted form of darkness. May all forms of human trafficking, or modern slavery, be eradicated from our country and the entire world.[59] Intercede that freeing more people from slavery in our time will produce good fruit that builds individuals up and heals our land. "**Christ has liberated us to be free. Stand firm then and don't submit again to a yoke of slavery**" (Gal. 5:1, HCSB). Ask the Lord to guard everyone from inadvertently becoming an agent of oppression. If you know someone dealing with the effects of subjugation, petition specifically for that person now. In the wake of 2020 protests related to police brutality, part of 16th Street NW adjacent to this park has been named Black Lives Matter Plaza. Thank God the area by the White House has long been a space for both recreation and Constitutionally-protected protest. Pray that assembly here is meaningful and peace-loving.

L3. **Libraries**, from 1st to 3rd Streets SE between East Capitol St and C St SE (Metro: Red line, exit at Union Station or take Blue, Orange, and Silver lines to Capitol South)

The Library of Congress was inspired by Benjamin Franklin's earlier public collection in Philadelphia, formed by a bill John Adams signed, and shaped by Thomas Jefferson's vision for comprehensive resources to help inform Congress.[60] This institution conserves and interprets the world's largest library.[61] Its 1897 home is across from the John Adams Building, and the James Madison Building faces Independence Avenue SE. Unless you have done a productive, eight-hour day's work in a world-class research library like this one, it can be difficult to imagine the sustained focus of the atmosphere in their quiet reading rooms. The intense research conducted here has the potential to impact the world. Thank God for the materials constantly being gathered to keep our country informed. Lift up Americans' attentiveness to forms of study that may help them grow in faith and closeness to God. Pray the Lord will increase our capacity to meditate on His Word. May we consistently open ourselves to spiritual cleansing and empowerment through sustained Scriptural study. While Paul was imprisoned, he stressed the importance of rigorous mental discipline: **"whatever is true, whatever is honorable, whatever is just, whatever is pure, whatever is lovely, whatever is commendable, if there is any excellence, if there is anything worthy of praise, think about these things"** (Phil. 4:8, ESV). Praise God for every work in this vast collection that encourages people to think about what is excellent and praiseworthy. Pray for all the living authors represented in the library's holdings. Intercede for the institution's staff along with every researcher and visitor accommodated in the past year.

The Folger Shakespeare Library celebrates how William Shakespeare's work has influenced American life. A couple founded the institution: Henry Clay Folger, a president of Standard Oil who retired a year before the 1929 market crash, and Emily Jordan Folger, a teacher and scholar of Shakespeare.[62] It has been well argued that Shakespeare drew from the painstakingly crafted Book of Common Prayer. Shakespeare's words have inspired intercessors to cite the theme of mercy from the Anglican Morning Prayer.[63] If this resonates with your faith tradition, I encourage you to echo one such model here. Portia, a voice of wisdom at the trial in *The Merchant of Venice*, provides one of Shakespeare's memorable references to interceding for mercy. She prompts reflection: "The quality of mercy is not strain'd, / It droppeth as the gentle rain from heaven … / It blesseth him that gives and him that takes … / And earthly power doth then show likest God's / When mercy seasons justice … in the course of justice, none of us / Should see salvation: we do pray for mercy; / And that same prayer doth teach us all to render / The deeds of mercy."[64] Pray that the Lord will pour out mercy. If there's something you need grace for right now, ask Jesus. If God would want you to extend His mercy to someone else in a particular situation, petition for the strength to obey and to show compassion.

L4. **Lincoln Memorial**, 2 Lincoln Memorial Cir NW (Metro: Blue, Orange, and Silver lines, exit at Foggy Bottom)

Going up the steps of the Lincoln Memorial places us on the Mall's long axis, which separates the capital's streets designated as North and South. The memorial's form was inspired by the Parthenon in Athens, using 36 exterior columns instead of the ancient model's 46 to signify each state in the Union when Lincoln was president.[65] All subsequent states have been added to its inscribed decoration, so this place offers an opportunity to pray for every part of the country as you feel led by the Holy Spirit. The interior's inscriptions reference the Gettysburg Address and Lincoln's Second Inaugural Address. This latter text shows his skill in calling for reconciliation: "with malice toward none; charity for all."[66] Thank the Lord for the measure of healing our country has experienced to date and for bringing many blessings through continued, if sometimes vigorously challenged, unity. Here, we remember how Lincoln proclaimed liberty on 1 January 1863: "all persons held as slaves … shall be then, thenceforward, and forever free."[67] Praise God that Lincoln emancipated slaves.

The seated colossal statue of Abraham Lincoln looks out over the National Mall. Consider mirroring his sculpture's perspective on D.C. by turning to face east under the portico. These steps provided the platform for Dr. King's "I Have a Dream" speech during a massive demonstration on 28 August 1963. Agree before the Lord with King's quotation that day from Amos 5:24 (WEB): **"let justice roll on like rivers, and righteousness like a mighty stream."** In this place, we remember that MLK's Dream Speech substantially built upon the ways that Lincoln's and Washington's work contributed to the cause of freedom in earlier times. One of the more immediate antecedents that set the stage for the Dream Speech, however, directly involved prayerwalking, or prayer marching, in the capital. The 17 May 1957 Prayer Pilgrimage for Freedom mobilized more than 30,000 nonviolent prayer warriors to honor, at these steps, the third anniversary of the Brown v. Board of Education school desegregation ruling.[68] This large Civil Rights demonstration gave Dr. King his first opportunity to speak before a national audience. Thank God for the sacred harvest America has already gathered as a result of prayerwalking in the capital. Pray that the Lord would multiply spiritual fruit from any seed planted to promote deliverance, reconciliation, and freedom. May God empower those who work today to overcome injustice through peaceful means. Ask the Holy Spirit to awaken many more individuals who **"shall raise up the foundations of many generations; … shall be called the repairer of the breach, the restorer of streets to dwell in"** (Is. 58:12, ESV). Intercede for people alive now who continue to extend the liberating work of Lincoln and MLK. May they be given the wisdom, energy, hope, and resources they need to continue every initiative anointed by the Lord.

L5. **Louisiana Avenue NW** (Metro: Red line, exit at Union Station)

While walking along Louisiana Avenue by Capitol Hill, remember the expansive New World territory that once formed the French colony that gave its name to this street. America's acquisition of the Louisiana Territory, stretching from the Gulf of Mexico up the Mississippi River and westward, significantly contributed to the vision of uniting areas between the Atlantic and Pacific Oceans into our large Republic. This land deal opened vast areas of the interior to increased trade and settlement via immigration. Consider the challenges and unjust situations that accompanied the country's westward expansion, praying specifically for the many displaced Native Americans whose tribes may or may not enjoy federally-recognized sovereign status today. Praise God for the rich cultural heritage of Louisiana, a state that offers something unique among the array of diverse American experiences. Thank the Lord for the variety of freedoms available before the Civil War to specific minority groups in this southern state. Rejoice with the people of Louisiana for considerable development there recently, even if much of it is associated with rebuilding after storms. Reflect on issues surrounding the topics of building and restoring that seem most pressing now. Lift up those who are directly engaged in these efforts, echoing the Prophet Isaiah's hope for positive change: **"they will restore the former devastations; they will renew the ruined cities, the devastations of many generations"** (Is. 61:4, HCSB).

M1. **Martin Luther King, Jr., Memorial**, 1964 Independence Ave SW (Metro: Blue, Orange, and Silver lines, exit at Smithsonian)

On a direct line between the Jefferson and Lincoln Memorials by the side of the Tidal Basin, we find the Rev. Dr. Martin Luther King, Jr., Memorial. The figural, thirty-foot sculpture finished in 2011 represents King as a "stone of hope" from a "mountain of despair." It quotes his 1963 "I Have a Dream" speech, which referenced Jefferson's Declaration of Independence from the steps of Lincoln's memorial.[69] King's service to America came with extreme personal costs, which included unjust imprisonment and ultimately giving his life in 1968 for the struggle against inequality. On the north wall of his memorial, a striking quote manifests grace and power in suffering. He wrote of freedom while in the Birmingham, Alabama, jail: "Injustice anywhere is a threat to justice everywhere … Whatever affects one directly, affects all indirectly."[70] In this powerful quote, we hear echoes of God's question for the murderer Cain: **"Where is Abel thy brother?"** (Gen. 4:9, KJV) Adam's son wanted to pretend that he had no responsibility in this matter, but his bloodguilt followed him the rest of his life (Gen. 4:13-16). Ask the Lord gently to show you any times you have hurt others. Pray for the supernatural ability to admit and rectify the wrongs we have done, as far as we are able.

Reflecting on the problem of injustice, consider Scriptural precedent for helping those we have never previously met through Jesus' answer to the following question: **"who is my neighbor?"** (Lk. 10:29, WEB) Jesus told a parable about the Good Samaritan, a marginalized man who generously cared for a seriously wounded and destitute traveler (Lk. 10:30-37). Jesus closed the discussion with a call to action: **"Go and do likewise"** (Lk. 10:37, WEB). Jesus' immediacy is reflected in King's letter from Birmingham's jail: "We must use time creatively, and forever realize that the time is always ripe to do right."[71] King's high standard reminds me of James's Divinely-inspired benchmark for wrongdoing: **"Remember, it is sin to know what you ought to do and then not do it"** (Jas. 4:17, NLT). Lay this challenge before the Lord. Pray for the Holy Spirit to guide your thoughts, and listen to the ideas that come to mind. If there have been times in your life when you did not act on what you knew was right, confess and ask God to help you turn from sins of inaction. Intercede for anyone who was harmed by your silence or reticence, asking that the Lord would make them completely whole and able to thrive going forward. Petition the Lord to show you ways you can avoid the pitfall of negligence in this season of life. Not everything can be solved in an instant, so this form of obedience is an ongoing process. What is the next right thing you are in a position to do today, this week, this month, and this year? Write down the ideas that come to you, and pray for the strength to do good in a timely fashion.

M2. **Mayor's Office**, 1350 Pennsylvania Avenue NW (Metro: Blue, Orange, and Silver lines, exit at Federal Triangle)

D.C.'s license plate motto reminds us of an injustice suffered by the city's more than two-thirds of a million full-time residents: "End Taxation Without Representation."[72] Being directly administered by the federal government, past District inhabitants could not even vote for their own local leaders during most of the Federal City's first century. On 9 July 1846, Congress legislated to retrocede all of Virginia's land grant to D.C. and restore full voting rights for their state's constituents. This bill asserted that D.C.'s area west of the Potomac River exceeded the: "territory … necessary and proper" for the Federal government's seat.[73] Our capital's remaining residents only gained the right to vote for the President and Vice President after the Twenty-third Amendment was ratified in 1961.[74] This significantly improved their circumstances. Disenfranchisement is all the more blatant because D.C. residents number more than the inhabitants of Wyoming or Vermont. The Constitution set up D.C. as an administrative district, so it would take yet another amendment to give citizens who reside exclusively in D.C. proper congressional representation. The capital's citizens have no senators, yet the area clearly needs year-round inhabitants. Their delegate in the House of Representatives cannot vote on the floor. Thank God for the citizens' increased autonomy by comparison with past centuries. Pray as the Holy Spirit leads about this form of inequality. Intercede regarding appropriate future responses to the situation, remembering Paul's charge to the Philippians: "**Let each of you look out not only for his own interests, but also for the interests of others**" (Phil. 2:4, KJV). Petition on behalf of the Mayor, D.C.'s local officials, and their front-line workers. May this city navigate its specific challenges as well as possible. Lift up issues surrounding racial tensions, pervasive Federal presence, jurisdictional overlap, transportation and parking issues, tourist traffic, large areas with more offices than dwellings, and many part-year residents.

M3. **Meade Memorial**, 333 Constitution Ave NW (Metro: Green and Yellow lines, exit at Archives)

The George Gordon Meade Memorial, in front of the District of Columbia's U.S. District Court and U.S. Court of Appeals, honors one Union general who helped win the Battle of Gettysburg. This sculpture sets him among the allegorical figures of virtues associated with accomplished war heroes: Loyalty, Chivalry, Fame, Progress, Military Courage, and Energy.[75] Ask God to give greater measures of these virtues to every Service member fighting on behalf of America today. Thank the Lord for raising up leaders who ended our country's Civil War. Praise Him that America became stronger after eradicating one widespread form of slavery, which asserted a crucially important check on states' rights. Many made the ultimate sacrifice for this internal struggle to increase freedom. As Abraham Lincoln recognized in his Gettysburg Address, they "shall not have died in vain." With this line honoring the fallen, our sixteenth president subtly alluded to the fruitful, life-giving death and resurrection of Jesus that accomplished what no one else ever could: **"I do not set aside the grace of God; for if righteousness comes through the law, then Christ died in vain"** (Gal. 2:21, NKJV). Lift up those who seek or try to gain redemption through purely human efforts, as the Holy Spirit leads. May they grow stronger in faith and receive God's grace.

****

M4. **Mexican Embassy**, 1911 Pennsylvania Ave NW (Metro: Blue, Orange, and Silver lines, exit at Farragut West)

Moving much closer to the city center in the late 1980s, the Mexican Embassy significantly expanded its visibility. This embassy's design features a form of preservation, building around and above a couple of D.C.'s earliest structures. Two facades remain from the seven upscale houses constructed in 1796 on plots that Philadelphian General Walter Stewart bought.[76] The homes' excellent locations provided, at different times, a base for embassies, presidents, vice presidents, and generals. In fact, one of the seven homes sheltered President James Madison and First Lady Dolley Madison while the White House was rebuilt after the War of 1812. Praise the Lord for the ways that historic structures have facilitated survival in uncertain times. Thank God for those who have supported conservation that safeguards memory. Pray about the process of ongoing preservation efforts in the capital, as you feel led.

Remember our neighbor to the south, Mexico, before the Lord. Ask God to bless their country for, among other notable contributions, the billions of dollars of agricultural products they sell to America each year. Their exports amount to nearly half of our fruits and vegetables. Invite the Lord to continue sending them rain and abundant sunshine in season, while guarding their farmers from the problems of pests, blight, and fire. Intercede for protection during extreme weather situations, like hurricanes. Lift up leadership at all levels in Mexico. Petition that the Lord graciously protects the disadvantaged and vulnerable. Thank Him for the high levels of literacy in their country. Pray for more Mexicans to read the Bible regularly and meditate on its message. Repeat one of God's promises in Isaiah over them: "**For as the rain comes down and the snow from the sky ... and makes [the earth] bring forth and bud, and gives seed to the sower and bread to the eater; so shall My Word be that goes forth out of My mouth: it shall not return to Me void, but it shall accomplish that which I please, and it shall prosper in the thing I sent it to do**" (Is. 55:10-11, WEB). Request the blessing of encouragement for believers and Christian fellowships in Mexico. May they enjoy the fruits of their labors.

M5. Museum of the Bible, 400 4th St at D St SW (Metro: Blue, Orange, and Silver lines, exit at Federal Center SW)

The large, interactive Museum of the Bible celebrates the Book that has had the most profound and lasting impact on American culture. In centuries past, the Bible was often the only volume a family owned. Scripture has long served as an accessible, comprehensive tool to fight illiteracy. A recent study suggests that over sixty-seven percent of Americans say they would like to learn even more about the Bible.[77] Pray that learning from and about the Bible is never considered outmoded, despite the fact that educational trends continue to change. Reflect on the Bible's practical character, as Paul wrote: **"All Scripture is inspired by God and is useful to teach us what is true and to make us realize what is wrong in our lives. It corrects us when we are wrong and teaches us to do what is right. God uses it to prepare and equip His people to do every good work"** (II Tim. 3:16-17, NLT). Thank God for the witness that every quotation of the Bible provides, particularly when the Holy Spirit illuminates it. Praise Him for the Scripture incorporated into this museum's displays. Pray for more sustained study of God's Word in America. Lift up those visiting MOTB galleries this past year who have not yet read the entire Bible—may they be inspired to keep on reading.

N1. National Academies, 2101 Constitution Ave NW (Metro: Blue, Orange, and Silver lines, exit at Smithsonian or Foggy Bottom)

Abraham Lincoln signed the original charter for the National Academies of the Sciences, Engineering, and Medicine to create an independent scientific advisory body to report on policy solutions, encourage innovation, and confront challenges for the good of society.[78] May God give them foresight about how to focus their efforts so they can advise our government well, being **"ready in season and out of season"** (II Tim. 4:2, NKJV). Thank the Lord for every positive contribution that academy members have made during the past 150 years and counting. Remember entities under the academies' umbrella, such as the Gulf Research Program and Transportation Research Board, whose recommendations affect Americans every day. Ask God to inspire their varied work in ways that significantly benefit humanity.

N2. **National Air and Space Museum**, 600 Independence Ave SW (Metro: Blue, Green, Orange, Yellow, and Silver lines, exit at L'Enfant Plaza or Smithsonian)

The Smithsonian's National Air and Space Museum began with a collection of fine Chinese kites in 1876 and grew to highlight the history of aviation from the 1903 Wright brothers' flights to space exploration.[79] Its enormous sister facility is found in Chantilly, Virginia. Hebrews chapter twelve in *The Message*, a paraphrased version of the Bible, reminds us of the inspiration that innovators can bring: **"Do you see what this means—all these pioneers who blazed the way, all these veterans cheering us on? It means we'd better get on with it … and never quit!"** (Heb. 12:1, MSG) Intercede for the crowds who have visited in the past year as well as all the staff, curators, and donors who facilitate unique educational experiences. Pray for the safety of every commercial airline you can remember, along with plane manufacturers and major air travel hubs in the country. Ask the Lord to give alertness to every pilot, co-pilot, flight attendant, marshal, baggage handler, mechanic, aviation engineer, and traffic controller. If you know people in this field—including aviators in the armed forces—lift them and their families before God. Think of the most distant place you have ever flown, and petition the Lord to help that region. Looking forward, if you plan to fly somewhere in the future, pray about that place and whatever you might do there.

N3. **National Council of Negro Women**, 633 Pennsylvania Avenue NW (Metro: Green and Yellow lines, exit at Archives)

Since the National Council of Negro Women's founding in 1935 at the 137th Street YWCA in New York City, this organization has fostered cooperation among other national groups that support and empower African American women.[80] Persistence in their focused, collaborative efforts led this institution to the power center of D.C. Their forty-year president, Dorothy Height, has been recognized as a co-organizer who welcomed demonstrators to the 28 August 1963 March on Washington.[81] At that event on the National Mall, Dr. Martin Luther King, Jr., delivered his landmark "I Have a Dream" speech. The NCNW members in attendance may well have imagined their descendants participating in King's vision of future peaceful reconciliation: "I have a dream that one day … little black boys and black girls will be able to join hands with little white boys and white girls as sisters and brothers."[82] Ask God to continue to multiply this vision and the conviction that all are created equal. Pray for everyone who has been marginalized or oppressed. Affirm, along with King David, confident trust in God's concern for the disenfranchised: **"The LORD is a refuge for the oppressed, a stronghold in times of trouble"** (Ps. 9:9, NIV). Remember in prayer any specific women you know who have suffered from bigotry and those who have personally overcome forms of discrimination. Thank the Lord for the efforts of organizations that work to lift up our country's daughters, sisters, mothers, aunts, godmothers, and grandmothers.

N4. **National Gallery of Art**, from 3rd to 9th Streets between Constitution Ave, Pennsylvania Ave, and Madison Dr NW (Metro: Green and Yellow lines, exit at Archives)

Where Pennsylvania Avenue reaches the Mall, we see the Andrew W. Mellon Fountain. Mellon was a businessman, politician, collector, and philanthropist who served as Treasury Secretary through the 1920s.[83] His art collection and financial contributions were fundamental in establishing the nearby National Gallery of Art. Thank God for America's legacy of generosity that has increased access to fine art, bringing more aesthetic excellence into the lives of many people. Praise Him for gifts to the country's institutions that have encouraged liberality from other donors. May we remember: **"He who sows bountifully will also reap bountifully"** (II Cor. 9:6, WEB). Pray that Christians will continue to cultivate a more open-handed attitude toward the wealth and possessions God enables them to enjoy. Reflect in prayer on the most generous act you have ever witnessed. Invite the Lord to show you ways you can exhibit more generosity through gifts of time, attention, finances, and volunteer service. Write down any ideas that come to mind, and plan a specific deadline for acting in obedience to the Holy Spirit's prompting. Petition that more Christians will listen carefully to such Divine prompts and step out from their comfort zones to give from the heart.

Among the gallery's works on paper that are too delicate to display at all times, its collection includes the extensive Index of American Design. A rich sample of similarly representative objects can be seen at the Smithsonian's Renwick Gallery, dedicated to American arts and crafts. Praise God for creative designers who have improved our society's overall experience. Thank the Lord for American artists and their design work, particularly for the examples you know and appreciate most. Many objects exemplifying the best of American design are still resting in cabinets, attics, and other storage facilities. Ask the Lord to protect these treasures of our cultural heritage until they can find a sympathetic viewer or collector who understands their historic importance. May God guard Americans from unknowingly disfiguring or throwing away art work or crafts of museum quality. Pray for individuals skilled in design and craftsmanship today. Intercede specifically for those you know who work in pottery, glass, wood, textiles, needlework, or any other craft medium. Bring to mind a specific time when someone or something pointed your thoughts toward beauty and excellence. Consider how God promised to inspire creativity when He instructed Moses about preparing the Tabernacle and all its components: "**I have put wisdom in the hearts of all the gifted artisans, that they may make all that I have commanded you**" (Ex. 31:6, NKJV).

N5. **National Mall**, from 1ˢᵗ St to Ohio Dr and Constitution to Independence Avenues (Metro: Blue, Orange, and Silver lines, exit at Smithsonian)

Parkland marks our capital's centralized and expansive cultural complex. Surrounding the Mall, note our many museums. I hope that you will eventually have time to visit every museum here. Lift up all the people who have explored, worked at, and supported these world-class institutions this past year. Thank God for the privilege it is to enjoy visiting such places for free, especially since most Americans have limited access to superlative collections in our daily lives. The Prophet Daniel was identified among the exiled **"Children … skillful in all wisdom, and cunning in knowledge, and understanding science, and such as had ability … [to master] the learning and the tongue of the Chaldeans"** (Dan. 1:4, KJV) in preparation for a lifetime of high-impact service. Similarly, these sites cover an expansive sampling of human learning and help augment a broad cultural education. Ask the Lord to inspire those who pursue lifelong learning here. Prayerwalking can be done silently and respectfully, eyes wide open, within galleries as well as outside these institutions. There's no need to rush through this area of the itinerary, especially if you can profitably extend the process of identifying new prayer topics. Take some time to read the Word, listen for the Holy Spirit's promptings, and generate more ideas for intercession on your own.

N6. **National Museum of African American History and Culture**, 1400 Constitution Ave NW (Metro: Blue, Orange, and Silver lines, exit at Smithsonian or Federal Triangle)

The newest addition to the Smithsonian family, the National Museum of African American History and Culture, had been envisioned in the early twentieth century. It was finally founded in 2003 and opened during President Barack Obama's second term. The museum celebrates "values like resiliency, optimism, and spirituality" in the context of educating about global influences associated with African American culture(s).[84] Ask God to use this museum to increase optimism and perseverance. Thank the Lord for the country's willingness to acknowledge past collective wrongs in such a prominent way. Praise God for the progress made and for those who continue to advocate for a more perfect experience of equality throughout our country. Pray about the interpretations of spirituality in the museum's exhibits, as you feel led. Lift up African American Christians who are models of resilience and witnesses of the Lord's power. Reflect on God's promises for His spiritual children: "'**For I know the plans I have for you,**' says the **LORD**. '**They are plans for good and not for disaster, to give you a future and a hope. ... If you look for Me wholeheartedly, you will find Me**'" (Jer. 29:11 and 13, NLT). May those learning from this museum's educational resources be inspired by milestones in the struggle for freedom and fully embrace the Lord's purpose for their lives. Intercede for perpetually greater understanding of the fact that, no matter our external circumstances, "**where the Spirit of the Lord is, there is freedom**" (II Cor. 3:17, CSB).

N7. National Museum of the American Indian, Independence Ave between 3rd and 4th Streets SW (Metro: Blue, Orange, and Silver lines, exit at Federal Center SW)

The undulating façade of the Smithsonian's National Museum of the American Indian is refreshingly conspicuous, given D.C.'s typically block-like architecture. This recent structure significantly augments the exhibition space of its sister museum by Bowling Green in Lower Manhattan. Remember the Native Americans in this country. Pray for as many sovereign tribal bodies as you know, including the ones in your home state. Intercede for the resolution of long-standing disputes and for appropriate recognition of their rights. Thank Him for their communities' perseverance and for the legacies they are building today. May they benefit from the blessings of a strong family: "**Like arrows in the hands of a**

warrior are children born in one's youth" (Ps. 127:4, NIV). Petition for any Native Americans you personally know to enjoy the highest good. Ask the Lord to open hearts through revelations of mercy, peace, and freedom.

N8. **National Theatre**, 1321 Pennsylvania Ave NW (Metro: Blue, Orange, and Silver lines, exit at Metro Center or Federal Triangle)

The National Theatre, dating from the 1830s, has welcomed a wide variety of talent from marching bands to opera and Shakespeare's plays to Broadway shows. Lift up the people who have animated, led, staffed, and attended this theater's productions. Pray about how going to the theater can help broaden our perspective by temporarily entering fantasy worlds. Ask God to give us wisdom as we analyze what is placed before us: "**Be careful that no one takes you captive through philosophy and empty deceit based on human tradition, based on the elemental forces of the world, and not based on Christ**" (Col. 2:8. HCSB). A theater housed one of our country's tragic moments: the assassination of Abraham Lincoln. Perhaps catching unfortunate glimpses of his future, Lincoln had previously watched Shakespearean actor John Wilkes Booth interpret the warped and bitter character of Richard III.[85] Intercede that the Lord would spare one person who is headed toward a tragedy today. Pray for God to keep demonstrating His mercy and patience. Invite the Lord, whenever it will help produce the outcomes He desires most, to caution our hearts and forewarn us through any available means. May we never ignore the Holy Spirit's promptings.

N9. **Navy Memorial**, 701 Pennsylvania Avenue NW (Metro: Green and Yellow lines, exit at Archives)

The United States Navy Memorial Plaza was envisioned by the capital's urban planner, L'Enfant, to commemorate America's naval power. His dream was finally realized in the twentieth century. Flags flown over the memorial can be dedicated to particular Service members and commemorative plaques can be donated.[86] This installation regularly gives our troops and military families in the grieving process a well-deserved honor. May God comfort and bless those who participate in memorial practices here, particularly any families who gave a plaque or dedicated a flag this past year. If you know individuals who have lost a loved one because of a military attack or the ocean's might, lift them up now. Pray for those in peril at sea today, trusting that God is sovereign over the weather and every other danger that crossing an ocean involves. Jesus demonstrated such power, calming the wind and waves with His words: "**Peace, be still**" (Mk. 4:39, KJV). This event echoes an ancient Biblical song of praise to God: "**He makes the storm a calm, so that its waves are still**" (Ps. 107:29, WEB). We know God can intervene in desperate circumstances, just as He protected President George H.W. Bush from losing his life at sea in World War II. Petition God for many more miraculous rescue stories in the future. Ask the Lord to guide naval initiatives and bring our sailors safely back to a friendly harbor.

O1. **Oak Hill Cemetery**, 3001 R St by 30th St NW, Georgetown (Metro: Blue, Orange, and Silver lines, exit at Foggy Bottom)

The Oak Hill Cemetery was founded by Willian Corcoran—now resting here—who also established the Corcoran Gallery, which was recently dissolved in ways that strategically benefitted other D.C. arts and educational institutions.[87] This resting place is associated with notables from the Civil War era, including some whose bones were later moved to what have been considered more appropriate settings: President Abraham Lincoln's son Willie (†1862) and the Confederate president Jefferson Davis.[88] Remembering that folks from across the political spectrum were interred here, let's consider the commonalities we share with people who do not have the same opinions, values, and priorities. Invite God to give you a greater ability to appreciate similarities and reach out to others, based—at least in part—on the experience of loss that unites humanity. Pray about how you might respond in the next year to the following verse: "**God is our merciful Father and the source of all comfort. He comforts us in all our troubles so that we can comfort others. When they are troubled, we will be able to give them the same comfort God has given us**" (II Cor. 1:3-4, NLT).

O2. **Office of Management and Budget**, 725 17ᵗʰ St at H St NW (Metro: Blue, Orange, and Silver lines, exit at Farragut West)

The Office of Management and Budget supervises federal agencies' performance and oversees our federal financial plan, working toward each administration's specific policy and regulatory goals. Federal procurement and information technology are among the processes they use to implement executive branch priorities. If you can think of times when these functions affected someone you know directly, pray about that situation, perhaps by praising God for the significant power our government has to obtain key raw materials and finished products. The OMB has also been involved with the hundreds of Executive Orders our presidents have signed in the past thirty years. Ask the Lord to protect us from any potential instances of government overreach. King David, sending Uriah to the front line, instructed Joab in one infamous command: "**retreat from him, that he may be struck, and die**" (II Sam. 11:15, WEB). Thank God that such personalized orders would be completely illegal in our system. Reflect on at least one influential Executive Order you remember. Lift up those affected by its policies as the Holy Spirit leads you.

O3. **Office of Refugee Resettlement**, 370 L'Enfant Plaza by 9th and D Streets SW (Metro: Blue, Green, Orange, Yellow, and Silver lines, exit at L'Enfant Plaza)

The Office of Refugee Resettlement helps those seeking citizenship to put down roots and identify available resources that can help them thrive here.[89] Pray for each new person able to enter the United States this year. Ask God to bless their wellbeing, connections, activities, and finances as they work to recognize and practice positive ways to contribute to our society. May they give back to our communities from the abundance the Lord has given them: "**As each one has received a special gift, employ it in serving one another as good stewards of the manifold grace of God**" (I Pet. 4:10, NASB). Thank the Lord for preserving the lives of those who have fled war-torn areas and all who have survived persecution or abuse. Praise Him for the ability our country has to be generous and welcoming to many refugees. Lift up all the ministries, nonprofits, and individuals who help refugees with the process of settling in America. Intercede for God's will to be done in the lives of individual refugees who have settled among us.

O4. **Old Stone House, Georgetown**, 3051 M St NW, Georgetown (Metro: Blue, Orange, and Silver lines, exit at Foggy Bottom)

The Old Stone House of 1765 was built by colonist Christopher Layman. Predating the construction of the capital under the Constitution, this is the oldest building on its original spot in D.C.[90] The home, constructed by its woodworking landowner, reminds us of the days when everyone knew that Georgetown was named after an English king and not after our first president. The household's earliest inventory mentions two Pennsylvania Dutch Bibles among the Layman family's modest possessions. A cast iron stove was their most expensive item. Thank God for this vivid reminder of colonial and Revolutionary-era lifestyles. May more Americans find contentment in what they have already experienced and whatever they currently own. Considering the assets you would list for a complete inventory, pray about what you value most at this moment, strictly based on how you have invested your resources over time. Petition for the gift of simplicity to enjoy all you have now. Ask the Lord to help you focus on the essentials, such as keeping your household warm in winter and feeding your soul with God's Word. Think of a time when you felt like the Psalmist David: **"How precious to me are Your thoughts, God! How vast is the sum of them!"** (Ps. 139:17, NIV)

O5. **Organization of American States**, 200 17th St at Constitution Ave NW (Metro: Blue, Orange, and Silver lines, exit at Smithsonian or Farragut West)

The Organization of American States promotes cooperation among all countries and territories on the American continents, as one of the United Nations' regional organizations.[91] Pray for officials who work in and with OAS to improve diplomatic relationships throughout our hemisphere. Ask God to serve His purposes through this organization. Part of OAS's outreach activity includes the Art Museum of the Americas, the oldest institution dedicated to modern and contemporary Caribbean and Latin American art in the country. OAS's main concerns are highlighted through exhibitions and programming related to democratic representation, development, human rights, justice, and innovation.[92] Lift up the artists, designers, preparators, docents, curators, security, and all others associated with this institution. Thank the Lord for increased awareness of Central and South American artists' achievements today. May the unique voices this institution features help promote ideal manifestations of equality in our region. Consider some of the ways the Prophet Isaiah raised consciousness of upright support for others: "**Learn to do good. Seek justice. Help the oppressed. Defend the cause of orphans. Fight for the rights of widows**" (Is. 1:17, NLT). Intercede for at least one person you know who falls into the categories Isaiah highlighted.

****

P1. **Pershing Park**, between 14th and 15th Streets on Pennsylvania Ave NW (Metro: Blue, Orange, and Silver lines, exit at Metro Center or Federal Triangle)

Pershing Park honors a preeminent World War I hero who enjoyed a special status previously held by George Washington alone. John J. Pershing achieved an extraordinarily high military rank—General of the Armies—and kept American bands of soldiers together to demonstrate our contributions while we helped free Europe during the Great War.[93] Thank the Lord for those who have found unmistakable ways to track America's substantive impact. Praise Him for giving past generals wisdom to triumph in situations that increased individual freedoms for many. Lift up all our active generals, interceding for discernment and strength. While we celebrate and honor Pershing's clear victory in helping liberate Europe, we acknowledge that the right path is not always clear from within a wartime fog. As the Prophet Isaiah wrote: "**we wait for light, but behold obscurity; for brightness, but we walk in darkness**" (Is. 59:9, KJV). We humbly confess we do not always know what is best in the long run. It can be difficult to fathom what will create a lasting and positive legacy, so let's pray for God's purposes to be served.

P2. Post Office, 1200 Pennsylvania Ave NW (Metro: Blue, Orange, and Silver lines, exit at Federal Triangle)

The Benjamin Franklin Post Office is named for the founding father who was postmaster general under the Second Continental Congress from 1775-76.[94] Experienced in managing postal services under British colonial rule in Philadelphia, Franklin improved efficiency, regularity, and set standardized methods for determining postage rates. Thank God for the predictability of postal service in this country. Lift up all the people who work to collect, expedite, and deliver our letters and packages. Consider how much of the New Testament was written in letter form. Think of a beloved verse from these epistles. One of my favorites is: "**we are made right with God through faith**" (Rom. 3:28, NLT). Old Testament letters that brought major changes included the documents Ezra and Nehemiah used while bringing Israel's remnant back from exile in order to reestablish the Temple and rebuild the walls of Jerusalem (Ezra 1:1-4 and 6:1-12; Neh. 2:7-9). Another Biblical letter that brought joy was King Hezekiah's invitation for the tribes to come celebrate the Passover in Jerusalem (II Chron. 30:1). Reflect on the most significant piece of mail you ever sent or received. Share with the Lord in prayer why this experience was impactful. Whether that example is associated with delight or trouble, use it to deepen the personal content of your silent prayer as you walk.

Q1. **Quaker School**, 3825 Wisconsin Ave NW (Metro: Shady Grove—Glenmont Red line, exit at Woodley Park—Zoo; see map inset)

Since their personal safety could no longer be assured in England, pacifists known as the Society of Friends, or Quakers, organized and settled in Pennsylvania during the late 1600s. Philadelphia, the territory's most prosperous city on the Eastern Seaboard, was the birthplace of our country. Independence Hall is a monument to the city's essential role in supporting those struggling for freedom. Philadelphia has been a temporary home to our government at each stage, from the Revolutionary period through the Articles of Confederation to our current Constitutional system. Central D.C.'s Pennsylvania Avenue has been called America's Main Street. There we find institutions that affect the future for locals, folks across the country, and people throughout the world. The road linking the Capitol and White House understandably honors this autonomy-loving, Quaker-influenced settlement that became our second state. Willian Penn, the colony's founder, wrote in Pennsylvania's First Frame of Government's preface that one of governance's aims is "to cherish those that do well."[95] The Sidwell Friends School, inspired by Quaker traditions and their peace testimony, has famously welcomed the children of at least four presidents and many other dignitaries. Bless those who are learning to value and practice peaceful approaches to problem solving. May they earn great respect and fulfill the purposes God intends for their lives.

During any long version of this prayerwalk that includes residential areas, you might pass by other public or private schools that educate K-12 students. The Proverbs recognize children's season of life as critical for character development: **"Train up a child in the way he should go: and when he is old, he will not depart from it"** (Pr. 22:6, KJV). Pray for every local child currently building intellectual, moral, and relational foundations. May learning the fundamentals help prepare America's children with the skills they need to flourish. Ask the Lord to give their parents wisdom for each day. Lift up all educators and staff members making decisions that impact students' lives. Invite God to empower them to do their best and facilitate excellent learning outcomes. Intercede for the schoolchildren and teachers you know personally as you walk onward. Petition specifically for whatever might bless each one the most, according to God's perfect timing and sovereign will.

R1. **Red Cross**, 430 17th St at D St NW (Metro: Blue, Orange, and Silver lines, exit at Smithsonian or Farragut West)

   The American National Red Cross, founded in 1881 by Clara Barton, has worked side by side with our military and is well known for blood drives as well as disaster relief.[96] They have an extensive network that effectively brings aid to those facing challenging circumstances in our country and abroad. Thank God for the significant assistance the Red Cross provides because of its generous donors. Ask the Lord to multiply the resources of those who are helping, according to a Biblical principle: **"A generous person will prosper; whoever refreshes others will be refreshed"** (Pr. 11:25, NIV). This block even has a blood donation center. Bless the many blood donors they have recruited to assure appropriate supplies for hospitals as well as long- and short-term medical facilities. Praise Him for each person helped by the Red Cross this past year. Lift up the Red Cross's leadership, staff, and volunteers wherever they are today. May the Lord empower and supply their unceasing works of mercy.

S1. **Salvation Army**, 2626 Pennsylvania Ave NW (Metro: Blue, Orange, and Silver lines, exit at Foggy Bottom)

   Near the bridge across Rock Creek, the Salvation Army National Capital Area Command works to provide aid and spiritual guidance for those in precarious situations or bound by substance abuse.[97] This multi-faceted charitable organization offers feeding and housing assistance as well as career-building programs for people trapped in unemployment and homelessness. Pray for every person they have helped this year to comprehend their precious, eternal value. Request that each one abounds in hope and finds lasting joy without regret in Christ. Intercede for those you know who are, or have been, dependent on a controlled substance, facing food insecurity, or struggling to stay in proper housing. Ask God to strengthen their faith and lead them toward demonstrable, positive change as well as overflowing thankfulness. Invite the Lord to help people in your circle who are unemployed or underemployed. May God **"enlarge the place of [their] ... tent"** (Is. 54:2, WEB) and lead them wherever He has prepared. Pray that God blesses children the Salvation Army serves with specific spiritual gifts and life-sustaining material provision. Petition that each child would fully understand and embrace how infinitely the Lord cherishes them.

S2. **Security and Exchange Commission**, 100 F St NE (Metro: Red line, exit at Union Station)

The Security and Exchange Commission's history can be explored using a virtual museum, which offers perspectives on its role in financial regulation.[98] Thank the Lord for the SEC's efforts to combat corruption. Pray for our country to master the kind of equitable financial integrity that pleases God: "**The LORD detests double standards; He is not pleased by dishonest scales**" (Pr. 20:23, NLT). Lift up everyone among us who follows Biblical principles with respect to money, taxes, and investments. Petition that Christians would perpetually hold themselves to the highest standards of financial ethics. Praise God for those courageous enough to speak truth and expose fraudulent activity. If you know any individuals directly affected by cases of financial malfeasance, remember them specifically before the Lord.

S3. **Senate Offices**, 2 and 120 Constitution Ave NE (Metro: Red line, exit at Union Station)

The Russell and Hart Senate Office Buildings support all 100 senators with spaces that provide easy access to the nearby Capitol. Centralized offices help promote dialogue among senators as well as their staff. Pray for the senators from your state by remembering their health and relationships. Petition for increased wisdom and excellent stewardship. Ask that these leaders would faithfully represent the interests and will of their own constituents. Since it's always difficult to find the best solution for high-stakes challenges, let's earnestly seek the Lord's sovereign will. Intercede for the greatest good, regardless of our limited perspective, that the senators might help bring to pass. Lift up the next election. Ask with boldness, because we can always trust that the Holy Spirit will interpret our requests according to God's ultimate purposes. "**And the Holy Spirit helps us in our weakness. For example, we don't know what God wants us to pray for. But the Holy Spirit prays for us with groanings that cannot be expressed in words**" (Rom. 8:26, ESV). Invite the Holy Spirit to keep this promise and translate all your prayers for our country.

S4. **Small Business Administration**, 409 3rd St at D St SW (Metro: Blue, Orange, and Silver lines, exit at Federal Center SW)

While most of the sites listed on this prayerwalk are unlikely to disappear or change drastically, other places in the city center experience significant turnover, temporary interruptions, and closures. The less permanent parts of D.C. are also notable topics for intercession. From brick-and-mortar retailers or restaurants to food carts or souvenir vendors, many fall under the umbrella of the Small Business Administration. The SBA provides advice, loans for entrepreneurs, and help with certification for winning government contracts. Lift up the agency's leadership and their key initiatives as the Holy Spirit leads. One of the Bible's small-scale manufacturers was Paul, who made tents to help finance his extensive missionary journeys. Priscilla and Aquila, who settled in Corinth after their Jewish community was expelled from Rome, hosted Paul while they produced tents side by side for more than a year (Acts 18:1-3, 11, 18-19). Just as the SBA aims to support business owners, Priscilla and Aquila helped Paul with resources, and they gave gentle, timely advice to Apollos in Ephesus. This tentmaking couple, after hearing Apollos preach, **"took him home and explained the way of God to him more accurately"** (Acts 18:26, HCSB). Their efforts produced positive results, because Apollos continued in ministry and **"greatly helped those who had believed through grace"** (Acts 18:27, WEB). Pray for the budding and established small businesses in D.C. Ask God to help entrepreneurs throughout our country find the advice, staff, and resources they need to succeed and bless others through their businesses.

S5. **Smithsonian Institution**, from 7th to 12th St SW and 9th to 14th St NW on the Mall (see also N2, N6, N7, and Z1 [map inset]; Metro: Blue, Green, Orange, Yellow, and Silver lines, exit at L'Enfant Plaza or Smithsonian)

      Although some Smithsonian museums have separate entries in this itinerary, the cluster along our central Mall can productively be discussed together. One block by Jefferson Drive swells to house a cluster of Smithsonian Institution buildings, promoting knowledge and research through their large, comprehensive collection. The Arts and Industries Building, formerly called the National Museum, has exhibited Smithsonian objects from 1881.[99] The collections grew over time to fill the National Museum of American History and National Museum of Natural History across the Mall, the National Postal Museum, and the National Air and Space Museum (N2). The Smithsonian's fine art was primarily divided between the Hirshhorn Museum (see below), National Portrait Gallery, Renwick Gallery, Smithsonian American Art Museum, and Freer Gallery. Many of the early exhibits came from Philadelphia's 1876 Centennial International Exhibition, which honored our country's 100th anniversary of independence. Thank the Lord that we have seen more than 240 of America's birthdays to date. Praise Him for the ways that freedom has expanded in the intervening time. Consider the growth that this building represents. Remember Jesus' parable of the mustard seed: **"It is the smallest of all seeds, but it becomes the largest of garden plants; it grows into a tree, and birds come and make nests in its branches"** (Mt. 13:32, NLT). Pray about ways to invest in the future. Ask God to show you how He wants you to sow in this season.

The Smithsonian Castle is a Norman revival building designed by Renwick and completed in 1855.[100] Once housing Smithsonian collections, it now contains a visitor's center and administrative offices. The museum complex's founder, chemist and mineralogist James Smithson, was the Duke of Northumberland's illegitimate son. He studied at Oxford and traveled extensively but never visited the United States. He was in Paris during the French Revolution, which may have impacted his feelings toward America's former English colonies. After a peripatetic life of scientific pursuits as a citizen "of the world," he left his fortune to our government for the purpose of his namesake institution, dedicated to "the increase and diffusion of knowledge."[101] Praise God for his generosity, which provides so many educational and employment opportunities today. Thank the Lord for individuals who follow idiosyncratic paths that result in the multiplication of blessings for many others. Lift up every woman who has protected and nurtured a child born outside of marriage, remembering any individuals you know personally in this situation. Pray that the Lord would minister directly to those who might question their own origins, speaking to them in ways they will accept about His everlasting and unconditional love. May we gently and tactfully reinforce how God's Word speaks to every person: **"Your [God's] eyes saw my unformed body; all the days ordained for me were written in Your book before one of them came to be"** (Ps. 139:16, NIV).

When the door facing the National Mall is open, you can walk through the Castle, get a drink of water, use other indoor facilities, and exit going south into the Enid Annenberg Haupt Garden at the back. This area housed animals from the Smithsonian's zoo in the 1880s, but now it provides a refreshing break from the overwhelming amount of information one can learn throughout the museum's multi-site complex.[102] Crossing the formal garden, we are above the ceilings of the National Museum of African Art and the Sackler Gallery, which links to the similarly themed Freer Gallery above ground on your right. These institutions showcase treasures from the ancestral homes of many Americans today, featuring fine collections of Asian and African art. Praise the Lord for the diversity and richness of our society. Thank God for the opportunity to learn from people of many different backgrounds within our own communities. Invite the Holy Spirit to inspire and empower any attempts to foster cultural exchange. Rejoice over the many strong Christians in our country who have African and/or Asian ancestors. Pray God leads Christians of every background to develop more profound sensitivity and engage constructively with folks from various traditions. May the Lord give us wisdom to relate as winsomely as possible to individuals of different faiths.

The Hirshhorn Museum and Sculpture Garden was founded by Joseph Hirshhorn, who left school in New York at age thirteen to sell papers and saved up enough to become a stock broker at sixteen.[103] He started collecting soon after, amassing about 6,000 objects of modern or contemporary art for the museum's initial gift and doubling it in his eventual bequest. This fine collection is, therefore, a witness to individual dedication and generosity. Thank the Lord for blessing our country with many industrious and magnanimous people. Praise Him for the ways Americans in different lines of work have significantly augmented the cultural riches of this country. Pray that the Lord leads each of us to think about how to benefit others' lives and follow through. May God activate our youth to begin building legacies of generosity early in life, because many could create opportunities to do more than they are currently accomplishing. As Paul wrote to Timothy: **"Don't let anyone think less of you because you are young. Be an example to all believers in what you say, in the way you live, in your love, your faith, and your purity"** (I Tim. 4:12, NLT).

S6. **State Department**, 2201 C St at 23rd St NW (Metro: Blue, Orange, and Silver lines, exit at Foggy Bottom)

The angle of the Vietnam Veterans Memorial's "cut into the earth"[104] points like a wide arrow in the direction of the State Department. Although most of us would only encounter this department when applying for a passport or consulting foreign travel recommendations, this diplomatic arm of the government works to encourage "democratic values and ... a free, peaceful, and prosperous world ... by advancing the interests of the American people."[105] Since the Vietnam War did not involve any attack on U.S. soil, we might interpret our motivations for entering that conflict within the State Department's expansive specified goals. Ask God to give more wisdom, restraint, and humility to our diplomats and everyone associated with the State Department's work. Intercede for positive, mutually-beneficial breakthroughs in our relationships with countries around the world. Although one may reasonably doubt that enduring peace and justice are attainable through purely human effort, pray for the full measure of these lofty goals that can be realized in our time. Invite God to bless State Department officials who pursue godliness. Consider using the Apostle Peter's benediction that echoes part of an acrostic poem King David wrote (Ps. 34:12-14): **"If you want to enjoy life and see many happy days, keep your tongue from speaking evil and your lips from telling lies. Turn away from evil and do good. Search for peace, and work to maintain it"** (I Pet. 3:10-11, NLT).

S7. Supreme Court, 1 1st St at East Capitol St NE (Metro: Red line, exit at Union Station)

After the War of 1812, our temporary Old Brick Capitol stood where the U.S. Supreme Court is now.[106] Our government's judicial branch ultimately defers to the judgment of this body, currently presided over by nine justices appointed for life. Significant responsibilities and opportunities for lasting legacy present those at our highest court with many potential traps or temptations over time. Pray that God does ongoing, profound work in the lives of these individuals who wield considerable power over the legislature, president, and people of our country. Reflect on the individuals involved in the highest levels of our judicial procedures. Consider their character and the processes refining them right now. Intercede that they will continually manifest the fruit God's Spirit produces: "**But the fruit of the Spirit is love, joy, peace, patience, kindness, goodness, faithfulness, gentleness, self-control; against such things there is no law**" (Gal. 5:22-23, ESV). Ask that they be given a more selfless love for others. Pray for them to enjoy spiritual refreshment from a deep well of joy, peace, and patience. Invite the Lord to increase their ability to show kindness, goodness, and faithfulness. May they be given greater humility that manifests in consistent gentleness and an unwavering ability to demonstrate self-control. Request that God expands their capacity for wisdom, foresight, sound interpretation of texts, integrity, and compassion.

Thank the Lord for the Supreme Court decision that has made the biggest positive impact in your life. If you can think of a ruling that has had negative consequences for you or someone you know personally, lift that situation before the Lord. Pray over each case you know about from this year, remembering both the ramifications of those already decided and the potential of ones that will be ruled upon soon. Ask God to prepare the individuals concerned most with these cases' outcomes, so that they will find ways to thrive, no matter the circumstances. As Proverbs reminds us: "**People may plan all kinds of things, but the LORD's will is going to be done**" (Pr. 19:21, GNT). Intercede for the lawyers arguing before this court to do their most diligent and persuasive work. Petition God to guard every word and direct final decisions toward His sometimes mysterious purposes. Pray the Lord would illuminate the clerks and any other staff members who may help sway outcomes. May justice be served here.

T1. **Transportation Department**, 1200 New Jersey Ave at M St SE (Metro: Green line, exit at Navy Yard—Ballpark)

Just as the Patriarch Jacob, or Israel, and his family rode to Egypt in wagons to escape a severe famine (Gen. 45:17-28), moving people and resources from place to place continues to preserve and improve our lives. Request that leaders in the transport sector practice high-quality data analysis, solve ongoing problems in real time, and have wisdom for each day. May our leaders be like Joseph who anticipated potential issues, saying: "**don't quarrel on the way**" (Gen. 45:24, WEB). If the Department of Transportation headquarters seems too far from your personal itinerary while prayerwalking with this book, remember their work when you first notice the fruit of their efforts. One manifestation includes any form of airline travel. Ask God to bless those involved in air transit and shipping of all kinds, helping them operate with consistent excellence. Petition the Lord to protect everyone in the air today. If you spot a standardized shipping container for intermodal transport on trucks, trains, or ships, it represents efficiency standards that the department promotes. Pray for those who seek to increase returns on investment by optimizing distribution practices. Intercede that God directs us toward the best transport methods, improving profit margins to benefit workers, investors, consumers, and their communities. Our transportation agency also works to prevent illegal trafficking of alcohol and drugs. Lift up the many ways that controlled substances have affected folks in our country, from users to their family members and employers to anyone harmed in accidents involving substance abuse. Consider local agencies who help regulate transit, such as the D.C. Department of Motor Vehicles. Pray about the motorists, passengers, cyclists, and pedestrians sharing our roads today.

T2. Treasury Department / Internal Revenue Service, 1500 Pennsylvania Ave NW (Metro: Blue, Orange, and Silver lines, exit at McPherson Square)

Next to the White House, we find our Department of the Treasury. Intercede for the administration of our country's funds, as the Holy Spirit leads. Remember the Treasury Secretary and staff at all levels of this institution. Ask the Lord to promote people into leadership positions who exhibit a steady and reasonable approach. As the Proverb says: **"Wealth obtained by fraud dwindles, but the one who gathers by labor increases it"** (Pr. 13:11, NASB). May God grant Treasury officials wisdom and superlative resource management skills. Since the Internal Revenue Service is under this department's umbrella, almost every American has been directly affected by their activities. Those who invest in government bonds or have a mortgage are acutely influenced by the Treasury's current standards. Pray for the folks who are most vulnerable to unexpected changes in the department's newest policies. Invite the Lord to help us individually, and as a country, to generate more than sufficient resources to sustain a prudent lifestyle, invest for the future, and be generous toward others.

The IRS was established in 1862, when Lincoln was president. Its reach extended after the 1913 ratification of our Constitution's Sixteenth Amendment, passed by Congress and approved under President Taft, made it legal to collect taxes on any income. Reflect on a couple of imperial Roman tax collectors who were highlighted in the Gospels. Zacchaeus, a chief tax collector, changed his corrupt practice of systematically increasing tax bills after meeting the Lord. Jesus summed up His intent in singling out Zacchaeus: **"The Son of Man came to seek and to save the lost"** (Lk. 19:10, GNT). One of Jesus' twelve disciples, Matthew, quit tax collecting (Mt. 9:9-13). Lift up those who are involved in gathering taxes for our country, asking for their faith to be strengthened. Jesus was careful to pay the taxes required, even though His methods of obtaining payment were not typical. My favorite tax story in the Bible is set in Capernaum, where leaders expected Jesus to pay a temple tax (Mt. 17:24-27). He instructed Peter to catch a fish, which had a coin in its mouth, in order to pay taxes for both of them (Mt. 17:27). Jesus affirmed that it was lawful to pay taxes to the occupying Romans. After pointing out Caesar's portrait and inscription on the denarius, He said: **"give back to Caesar what is Caesar's, and to God what is God's"** (Mt. 22:21, NIV). Praise the Lord that our financial needs are not beneath Jesus' level of interest. Pray God will help Americans cultivate the transparency, organizational skills, and wisdom they need both to prepare and pay the taxes they lawfully owe in a timely fashion.

U1. **Union Station**, 50 Massachusetts Ave NE (Metro: Red line, exit at Union Station)

Locate the main entrance to Union Station on Columbus Circle, noting its grand exterior. Its façade recalls the Roman Imperial Arch of Constantine, finished by AD 315.[107] This architectural precedent references the Greco-Roman roots of our government with a specific caveat, because various triumphal arch motifs were available for the designer to cite. Constantine was the Roman emperor who ushered in significant religious tolerance with the 313 Edict of Milan and converted to Christianity himself.[108] Rejoice over this reminder of the event that outlawed official martyrdom of ancient Christians in the Roman Empire. Praise God that Rome's moment of protecting religious freedom has been tangibly honored via this specific architectural precedent in our capital. If you need water, food, or a restroom visit, the station is one place to stop. On the inside, find the list of regional trains ready to depart. Pray for each of the places mentioned. Paul's ministry focused on witnessing in cities. It all started with Paul's dramatic conversion, when Jesus directed him in a vision: "**rise up, and enter into the city, and you will be told what you must do**" (Acts 9:6, WEB). Ask for the Church to grow in cities linked to D.C. by rail. May God's love and forgiveness become more widely and personally known along this busy corridor. Intercede for those riding or overseeing rail traffic today. Thank God for the ease and sustainability of this transportation form. Praise the Lord for every train trip that has been completed without incident during the past year. If you know anyone affected by a railway disaster, pray about those specific circumstances now.

U2. **Unions**, 25 Louisiana Ave NW (Metro: Red line, exit at Union Station)

The Teamsters Union represents well over one million workers in a wide variety of occupations, from truck drivers to public defenders.[109] Lift up individuals directly involved with and affected by union policies. For instance, if you know children in the public school system, remember their unionized teachers. Solomon noted problems with isolation in the workplace that had manifested in his time: "**There is one who is alone, and he has neither son nor brother. There is no end to all of his labor…. Two are better than one, because they have a good reward for their labor. For if they fall, the one will lift up his fellow; but woe to him who is alone when he falls, and doesn't have another to lift him up**" (Eccl. 4:8-10, WEB). May American workers find the support they need to be as productive and safe as possible while they make positive contributions to our society. Petition for our country to continue aiming toward excellence with respect to workers' rights. Intercede for every union member or union leader you know, according to their particular situations. Ask God to bless them in specific ways they might never have imagined or requested. Pray that we would more deeply appreciate the Lord's supernatural perspective and ability to provide, remembering: "**your Father knows what things you need, before you ask Him**" (Mt. 6:8, WEB).

U3. **United States Trade Representative**, 600 17ᵗʰ St NW (Metro: Blue, Orange, and Silver lines, exit at Farragut West or McPherson Square)

In 1962, John F. Kennedy established this agency to develop trading policy, negotiate agreements, and coordinate trade practices within the government. Participating in the World Trade Organization, the USTR also maintains offices in Geneva and Brussels. Their policies help regulate the flow of goods between our 50 states, U.S. territories, and roughly one-third of the world's countries. Ask the Lord to bless the Trade Representative, USTR officials, and all their counterparts abroad with increasing foresight and strategic cooperation. Intercede regarding the challenges associated with these high-stakes negotiations. Thank Him for the ways trade with other countries helps improve our quality of life. Lift up those who work to make the most of our country's resources through fair and timely trade deals. The woman of noble character in Proverbs is known for a similarly expansive view of household management: "**She is like the merchant ships, bringing her food from afar. … She sees that her trading is profitable, and her lamp does not go out at night**" (Pr. 31:14 and 18, NIV). Reflect on something you recently obtained from a foreign source, and pray the Lord blesses all those involved in making that product available. If you have ever produced something that was sold in more than one country, praise God for the opportunities our country's trading deals have facilitated.

U4. **University**, 37th and O Streets NW, Georgetown (Metro: Blue, Orange, and Silver lines, exit at Foggy Bottom)

Georgetown University is the country's oldest Catholic institution of higher learning, associated with the Jesuits' charisma for teaching. On 37th Street, between N and O Streets NW, find its gated lawn with signs that draw our attention to time and truth. Note Healy Hall's clock tower looming directly ahead. May the Lord order the university community's hours in ways that allow each person opportunities and mental space to think beyond themselves. Ask God to help D.C. scholars with increasingly efficient time management. Pray that students will discern how best to structure their studies. Remember Solomon's saying: "**A man's heart plans his course, but Yahweh directs his steps**" (Pr. 16:9, WEB). Invite God to keep whispering the reality of forgiveness, grace, salvation, healing, and deliverance through Jesus into the thought lives of those on campus. Acknowledge the Lord is able to do much more than this. The horizontally-articulated library façade along the south side of this greenspace has a central window revealing an interior inscription in Latin, which translates: "**you will know the truth, and the truth will set you free**" (Jn. 8:32, BSB). Request that God will continue showering blessings linked with Biblical truth on people associated with all faith-based universities in the country. Intercede that every friendship and marriage bond forged on campus will serve God's purposes. Lift up students, staff, and instructors who are open to faith's relevance in scholarship as well as those pursuing work that focuses on Christian content.

V1. **Veterans Affairs Department**, 810 Vermont Ave near H St NW (Metro: Blue, Orange, and Silver lines, exit at McPherson Square)

Just northeast of the White House, the Veterans Affairs Department headquarters is on Vermont Avenue between Lafayette and McPherson Squares. Its location reminds us that more than two-thirds of our country's presidents have served in the armed forces. Among those who became our military's Commander-in-Chief, most had interrupted civilian careers to fight for America. In recognition of our former troops' high potential to contribute beyond their military service, the Department of Veterans Affairs facilitates many programs intended to improve vets' prospects. One famous example is the GI Bill, which was designed to fund training, tuition, housing, and supplies for students who are vets. Recipients can also qualify as a veteran's spouse or child. Praise the Lord for every generation that has benefitted from this help since the GI Bill's initial version in 1944. May this program continue to bear excellent, lasting fruit. As the Proverb exhorts: "**Keep hold of instruction; do not let go; guard her, for she is your life**" (Pr. 4:13, ESV). Thank God for the many opportunities that this educational assistance has provided. Pray for VA leadership and staff at every level, especially as they adapt offerings to the greatest needs of this moment. Other VA programs include healthcare, debt management, anti-homelessness initiatives, and vocational rehabilitation.[110] Intercede for veterans and their family members who take advantage of VA programs this year, as the Holy Spirit leads. If you know anyone personally involved with VA initiatives, petition for God's best in that specific case.

V2. **Vice President / Naval Observatory**, 3450 Massachusetts Ave NW (Metro: Shady Grove—Glenmont Red line, exit at Woodley Park—Zoo; see map inset)

Observatory Lane NW leads to one of the country's oldest scientific institutions. I encourage you to stay respectfully on either Wisconsin or Massachusetts Avenues while praying for this active military installation. The Naval Observatory was originally a few streets north of the Lincoln Memorial, but it was moved here in the 1890s to expand their ability to research astronomy and oversee exact time measurement.[111] Pray about your stewardship of time as you continue, petitioning for wisdom to be responsible with the time you are given. Reflect on Paul's reminder: "**Therefore watch carefully how you walk, not as unwise, but as wise; redeeming the time, because the days are evil**" (Eph. 5:15-16, WEB). This institution has hosted scientists who made achievements in discovering Mars's satellites and monitoring the sun's activity. Praise the Lord for ordering the world to enable accurate navigation through traditional low-tech time keeping methods and basic astronomical observation. Thank Him for the Navy's ability to plan and execute precise maneuvers that have supported the freedom of millions over time. Ask God to bless scientists with excellence in their research and give them the capacity to envision many practical applications to benefit our communities. Pray that someone will take time to look intently up at the stars tonight and think about big questions.

One Observatory Circle is the Vice President's official home. This position typically attracts team players who understand the value of working with others and can handle letting another person take credit for successes. Key aspects of the job remind me of the faith-filled centurion, who told Jesus: "**I also am a man under authority**" (Mt. 8:9, NASB). As we remember our Vice President, intercede for this public servant's health and family. Lift up any pressing safety concerns. Request that the Lord directs the Vice President's paths. May God continue to draw trustworthy staff and advisers to help our VP fill an essential supporting role.

V3. **Vietnam Veterans Memorial**, 5 Henry Bacon Dr NW between the Mall's Reflecting Pool and Constitution Ave (Metro: Blue, Orange, and Silver lines, exit at Smithsonian or Foggy Bottom)

The Vietnam Veterans Memorial, a profoundly elegant design by Maya Lin, enshrines the names of over 58,000 missing or deceased Americans who served in Vietnam. Read at least a few of the names as you respectfully follow the path, lifting up the loved ones who survived them. While contemplating so many losses is always sobering, experiencing this monument is never exactly the same. Visitors regularly place memorial objects at the base of the wall. The National Park Service carefully collects these objects to preserve or dispose of them at their discretion, conserving parts of the grief process for individuals lost during a controversial war to help recognize this conflict's ongoing historical value.[112] Pray for those mourning here, as you would want an outsider to remember your own family in a time of loss. If you can, "**weep with those who weep**" (Rom. 12:15, WEB). Thank the Lord for stopping this war that was cruelly prolonged by a leader who probably killed over one hundred thousand of his own North Vietnamese people. Praise God for the Service members who returned from this war. If you know anyone directly affected, from a soldier or official to a refugee, intercede for that person specifically now. Invite the Holy Spirit to help our leaders resolve more prisoner-of-war and missing-in-action cases. Just as the path begins to rise toward ground level, look around to notice how the memorial's arms lead our eyes toward both the Washington and Lincoln Memorials. Find the nearby *Vietnam Women's Memorial*, which acknowledges contributions to the fight that have sometimes been overlooked. May we never forget sacrifices made for our country.

W1. **Washington Monument**, 2 15th St NW on the Mall (Metro: Blue, Orange, and Silver lines, exit at Smithsonian)

Washington's massive obelisk is inscribed "Praise be to God" (Laus Deo) on top, reminding us to glorify the one true God.[113] Exalt the Lord in your own words here. The Mall's crossing point is marked by a 555-foot stone tower honoring our country's first president.[114] On 23 August 2011, it sustained serious damage during a 5.8 magnitude earthquake, the epicenter of which was just ninety miles away.[115] Thank God there were no life-threatening injuries at the monument as a result of the quake. This raised area of the Mall gives us a singular perspective on L'Enfant's original plan and refinements introduced by other designers, such as Olmstead. The form of this monument is derived from pharaonic Egypt, which included obelisks in temple complexes built by autocratic rulers. Such monuments were once exclusively associated with the slavery-dependent ancient empire. Genesis accounts show that, during a crushing famine, "**Joseph reduced the [Egyptian] people to servitude**" (Gen. 47:21, NIV) to preserve their lives. Eighty-two-foot obelisks from the Luxor temple, underwritten by Ramses II, now stand at the original site in Egypt and at the Place de la Concorde in Paris.[116] Clearly, this form's connotations have expanded, because obelisks prominently mark the capitals of more than one republic. In D.C., it stands in for the imposing figure of George Washington, who led effectively in war and peace. Washington helped start the process of liberation in America by confronting colonial tyranny. When we look south to the Jefferson Memorial, we remember how another founder-president from Virginia similarly helped liberate our country from colonial oppression. Turning west to the Lincoln Memorial, we are reminded that the Unifier-in-Chief brought emancipation to many enslaved Americans. The struggle for liberty continues, because slavery—human trafficking—exists in modern forms now. Thank God for the courage, diligence, and vision of our founders and first president to begin a process of expanding freedom that continues today.

The Washington Monument is a good place to recall attacks and losses, whether actual or intended, and compare them with America's tenacity to rebuild. When we turn north and east, respectively, we see the grand versions of the White House and Capitol buildings that were rebuilt after the British burned D.C. during a wartime attack in 1814.[117] Many have suggested that one hijacked plane on 9/11 was intended to hit the Capitol, but the determined passengers and flight crew grounded it in Shanksville, Pennsylvania.[118] A memorial has since been established in honor of the individuals lost in that crash. Praise God for empowering people to help circumscribe casualties on 9/11 by heroically limiting the destructive potential of United Flight 93 in an unpopulated area. We remember their sacrifice and lift up their survivors before the Lord. Pray for God to continue to protect us, according to His perfect will. Ask the Lord to heal our country's wounds. May God always give us grace to forgive and strength to help restore our communities. Remember how Flight 93 hero, Todd Beamer, and phone operator, Lisa Jefferson, prayed during the flight's final minutes.[119] Let's likewise intercede using the Lord's Prayer: "**Our Father which art in heaven, Hallowed be Thy name. Thy kingdom come. Thy will be done in earth, as it is in heaven. Give us this day our daily bread. And forgive us our debts, as we forgive our debtors. And lead us not into temptation, but deliver us from evil: For Thine is the kingdom, and the power, and the glory, forever. Amen**" (Mt. 6:9-13, KJV).

W2. **White House**, 1600 Pennsylvania Ave NW (Metro: Blue, Orange, and Silver lines, exit at Farragut West, McPherson Square, or Metro Center)

A clearing in the greenspace at 1600 Pennsylvania Avenue brings the White House into view. An entire prayer marathon could be devoted to all the people, daily functions, events, and historical background associated with our executive residence. Being selective, we will focus on the President, White House staff, media representatives, and the building itself. Let's first lift up anyone animating its spaces—regularly or temporarily—who follows the advice of King Solomon: "**Trust in the LORD with all your heart; do not depend on your own understanding. Seek His will in all you do, and He will show you which path to take**" (Pr. 3:5-6, NLT). Pray that individuals who trust God and seek Divine wisdom always have influence here.

Multiple façade elements bring to mind the White House's range of functions, which invite prayer. Its main upper level is residential. Intercede for the current President and First Spouse as well as their children and extended family. Invite God to grant them wisdom for each moment and empower them to do what is best. The roof reminds us of those who constantly monitor the grounds, interior, and air space. Remember everyone protecting the First Family. May they be consistently vigilant, discreet, and above reproach. The wings, added during the twentieth century, speak to the variety of daily governmental duties essential to the institution. Ask God that each member of its complex team will work with unfailing excellence and a constructive attitude. Bless each person providing for the practical needs of the home's residents, staff, and guests, who include dignitaries, officials, aides, press, and tourists. May their work be a source of fulfillment. Thank the Lord this house is typically open for public tours, honoring the way it runs on revenue from tax payers. Praise Him for the times this facility has comfortably accommodated the most elite diplomatic functions that aim to foster good relationships with foreign rulers, diplomats, governors, representatives, and leaders in various domains. Intercede for the janitorial staff, maintenance, and gardeners who take care of important details and help make life more beautiful here.

Signs from the home's exterior speak to its essential outreach functions. From a vantage point by the North Lawn, we can see the 1870s fountain that President Ulysses Grant contributed to the ensemble.[120] From the window above its northern door, President Lincoln once addressed crowds that gathered on the lawn by the thousands. Although this area is now off-limits for anyone without a pass, it is good to remember that leaders have worked to demystify this institution and welcome the people. Access in our own day is usually mediated by local, national, independent, and international press outlets. You may see groups of network anchors and camera operators on the lawn. Petition the Lord to direct their words, consciously or unconsciously, in ways that serve His purposes. May everyone who listens to their reports have wisdom to figure out what is really at stake and where potential biases lie. Pray for discernment whenever citizens hear differing perspectives: "**The words of a man's mouth are like deep waters. The fountain of wisdom is like a flowing brook**" (Pr. 18:4, WEB). Ask that we see clearly, like Solomon: "**The purposes of a person's heart are deep waters, but one who has insight draws them out**" (Pr. 20:5, NIV). Reflect on your impressions of the White House's efforts to communicate and govern, requesting better understanding of any novel policies that apply to your own season of life and sphere of influence.

Designed by the architect George Washington chose, the White House's neoclassical style emulates precedents from ancient Greece and Rome. Since these ancient civilizations—in specific ways and at certain times—incorporated voting into their political systems, this style recalls the importance of representation for our self-governing country. Just as the ancient Greeks' definition of democracy limited suffrage to free male landowners, our founders did not immediately allow all individuals the right to vote. Thank God that, in the intervening time, amendments have been passed to extend voting rights to every adult citizen. Pray for all our citizens to fulfill their civic duties and vote.

Reflecting on virtues can inspire prayer for everyone who lives and works at the White House, remembering especially its dedicated Cabinet member, the Chief of Staff. Ask the Lord increasingly to build virtues into the minds and hearts of individuals at the center of our government's executive branch. May virtues abound at all levels of those involved with executing our country's laws from policy makers to police. Intercede for each person's character more consistently to manifest prudence, fortitude, temperance, and justice. Petition that they all be given stronger faith, hope, and love to serve our country to the best of their abilities. Let's pray to be inspired in like manner: "**Three things will last forever—faith, hope, and love—and the greatest of these is love**" (I Cor. 13:13, NLT). Invite the Holy Spirit to encourage a dependable atmosphere of self-control, humility, and diligence at the White House. May each person associated with executive branch leadership embrace and exhibit these lofty ideals of character.

W3. **World War II Memorial**, 1750 Independence Ave SW (Metro: Blue, Orange, and Silver lines, exit at Smithsonian)

The 2004 World War II Memorial occupies the eastern end of the long reflecting pool in front of the Lincoln Memorial. The multi-front, coordinated effort to respond to the Japanese attack on Pearl Harbor and liberate Europe from Fascism is remembered with stone canopies designating both Pacific and Atlantic theaters. The names of all U.S. states and territories grace granite piers surrounding a fountain and framing a curved wall with over 4,000 stars that symbolically honor the 405,399 Americans who died while serving.[121] They include sixty-six casualties from among the famous Tuskegee airmen—Black pilots who were collectively decorated for excellence.[122] About sixteen million soldiers completed the war's complex campaign in less than four years. Praise the Lord for their dedication, modeling a special kind of faithfulness that mirrors how Paul once exhorted Timothy: "**Share in suffering as a good soldier of Christ Jesus. No soldier gets entangled in civilian pursuits, since his aim is to please the one who enlisted him**" (II Tim. 2:3-4, ESV). Thank God for directing the outcome of this war to preserve America's sovereign territory and stop Hitler. Intercede for all living veterans. Remember surviving family members of deceased Service members. Walk around the entire memorial, reading each state or territory's name to yourself. Lift up these places, as you feel led. When you see your home state's name, pray for your governor, lieutenant governor, elected congressional and state representatives, local leaders, police, firefighters, hospitals, schools, and houses of worship.

X1. **XFL D.C. Defenders**, Audi Field, 100 Potomac Ave at R and 2nd Streets SW (Metro: Green line, exit at Waterfront or Navy Yard—Ballpark)

Not far from the Anacostia River, we find Audi Field, which hosts the D.C. United Soccer Club that was founded in the 1990s. Thank God for the ways American sports have expanded in the past thirty years and encouraged fitness goals. This venue had been slated to welcome the Spring 2020 revival of the XFL football league. The D.C. Defenders were deprived of a full season, due to policies associated with the COVID-19 pandemic. The virus closed down their league and prompted bankruptcy filing in April 2020.[123] Ask God to continue helping people whose jobs were mandated to stop during the pandemic and whose companies shut down completely. Intercede for them using one of the blessings the Prophet Jeremiah recorded: "**blessed are those who trust in the LORD and have made the LORD their hope and confidence. They are like trees planted along a riverbank, with roots that reach deep into the water. Such trees are not bothered by the heat or worried by long months of drought. Their leaves stay green, and they never stop producing fruit**" (Jer. 17:7-8, NLT). Pray that God will sustain them through the recovery process by helping them adapt and make the most of available opportunities. Lift up everyone in positions to help Americans who recently lost their jobs. Petition the Lord that they will have wisdom to open up substantive prospects and strategically put additional resources into circulation. Although this site is not currently associated with playing American football, it offers us a chance to remember those who play, support, and watch live sports. May athletes whose careers have been disrupted continue training in ways that promote optimal health and prepare them to thrive in their next positions, whether on or away from the field.

Y1. **YMCA**, 1112 16th St at L St NW (Metro: Red, Blue, Orange, and Silver lines, exit at Farragut North or McPherson Square)
Y2. **YWCA**, 1020 19th St between K and L Streets NW (Metro: Blue, Orange, and Silver lines, exit at Farragut West)

The Young Men's Christian Association (1844) and Young Women's Christian Association (1855) operate multiple sites in D.C. These long-standing ministries, started in England, have adapted over time to help many people throughout the world. They impact lives from London to Nairobi, Jerusalem to Shanghai, and Buenos Aires to Auckland. Their outreaches have traditionally focused on spiritual encouragement, education, physical fitness, temporary accommodation, and employment assistance.[124] May they foster healthy friendships and help individuals pursue excellence. Pray about how Paul summarized his devotion to obeying the Lord using a sports reference: "**So I run straight toward the goal in order to win the prize, which is God's call through Christ Jesus to the life above**" (Phil. 3:14, GNT). From 1861, YMCA volunteers reached out to troops on the battlefield, leading the United Services Organizations' relief efforts for our soldiers in the 1940s.[125] Intercede that the "Y" will continue to benefit people—at home and abroad—who seek guidance as well as healthy forms of fellowship. Ask the Lord to bless whoever remains among original USO participants, as you feel led by the Holy Spirit: YMCA, YWCA, National Catholic Community Services (suspended in the 1980s), Jewish Welfare Board, Salvation Army, and the National Travelers Aid Association (now Travelers Aid International). Petition God that their legacy of service to the country will inspire others to be hospitable and generous.

Z1. **Zoo**, 3001 Connecticut Ave NW (Metro: Shady Grove—Glenmont Red line, exit at Woodley Park—Zoo; see map inset)

Whether you prayerwalk silently through the zoo at Rock Creek Park or not, request Divine protection to cover everyone here today. Ask God to continue giving wisdom to the zoologists, handlers, and administrative staff to steward the animals in their care. Especially if you enter the park, pray through the functions and/or themes related to different animals.[126] For instance, at the children's farm exhibit, you might thank God for the alpacas' warm fleece we can use as clothing. If you want to focus on more abstract themes, you might intercede for leaders when you see the lions and tigers, who occupy the food chain's apex. God's plan for animals includes the universal mandate: **"Be fruitful and increase in number and fill the water in the seas, and let the birds increase on the earth"** (Gen. 1:22, NIV). Praise the Lord for every animal that thrives in our time. May they fulfill this directive to increase. Remember those who have the power to protect endangered animals, asking for God's will to be done. Invite the Lord to help any person who is suffering now as a result of unhealthy contact between animals and humans. One infamous example is plague, a treatable illness that experts have associated with transmission from an infected flea to a person.[127] Pray about animals that facilitate catastrophic health issues, like disease-carrying mosquitos infecting people with malaria, dengue fever, Zika, EEE, and other serious illnesses in many parts of the world. Petition for yourself and all fellow prayerwalkers to be safeguarded against animal bites from threatened strays or unleashed pets. May God help us do our best as stewards of the animal kingdom.

****

Conclusion: A Look Back

Facing east from the Lincoln Memorial steps (see map: L4), think about all the core elements of American government and review some major prayer topics. The Washington Memorial reminds us of the executive branch, recalling George's measured wisdom to focus first on fighting colonial oppression in order to win independence (W1). There's no doubt that more people in America were free from subjugation at the end of his life than at its beginning. Washington's efforts enabled subsequent leaders to address different, weighty problems. Further expansion on their collective, positive contributions over time is helping us create a more perfect union today. The Capitol's façade clearly articulates work shared by both House and Senate in the legislative process (C2). This massive building also evokes our system's intended balance of powers. If we could elevate our perspective by 1,000 feet, we would see the Supreme Court behind the Senate wing of the Capitol and bring our judicial branch to mind (S7). East of the House of Representatives' assembly space, we would find the Library of Congress that collects and preserves resources to inform all three branches in their mandates to serve their constituents (L3). Bringing our mind's eye back down, the shimmering waters of the Reflecting Pool and green expanse of the National Mall recall the well-watered land we share (N5).

Straight ahead, we see the Capitol's west façade, where presidents traditionally take the oath of office and give an inaugural address at the top of the steps. Pray about what it would mean, according to your season in life, for you to echo our official oath to "preserve, protect, and defend the Constitution of the United States."[128] How is the Lord leading you to defend, in your own particular situation, the ideals of life and liberty? Reflect before God on John F. Kennedy's resonant words: "And so, my fellow Americans: ask not what your country can do for you—ask what you can do for your country."[129] May the Lord embolden everyone in a position to do something that could benefit our country today. Invite God to give us wisdom and strength to make an impact for good. Ask the Lord how He wants you to serve your family, community, and country. Pray that you will be faithful to continue lifting America before God. Let's echo the Prophet Samuel's commitment to Israel as we promise the Lord to intercede regularly for our own country: "**As for me, I vow that I will not sin against the LORD by ceasing to pray for you**" (I Sam. 12:23, HCSB).

Notes
****

Notes

****

Notes

****

Notes

****

Notes
****

Notes
****

Notes

****

Contributors

Margaret Hadley began the dedicated practice of interceding for our country over twenty-four years ago, while she interned at one of the Smithsonian museums in D.C. Purposefully focusing her mind on the Lord and His kingdom during lengthy walks—collectively covering much of the Federal City—encouraged her faith and strengthened her hope that true freedom is possible for all. Experiencing the quiet joys of prayerwalking and seeing clear answers to prayer inspired her to share this approach to intercession. Her research on episodes in the history of prayer has been published on both sides of the Atlantic, presented at professional conferences, and shared with university students.

Millie Kuehnast is an experienced illustrator currently working toward a Bachelor of Fine Arts degree. For more of Millie's work, see: millustrationsart.wordpress.com. Since completing her first publication, *A Prayerwalk Around Paris's Central Islands* (2018), she has branched out into digital art. Working with Photoshop and a drawing tablet facilitated this book's clean, detailed style. Entering senior year on the dean's list, she will graduate in 2021 with a major in Graphic Design and a minor in Illustration. Her ultimate goal is to glorify God, and she continues to follow where He leads.

Index of Nearby Metro Stations

Archives: A2, C1, F2, F3, L1, M3, N3, N4, N5, N9
Arlington Cemetery: A1
Capitol South: B1, B3, H5, L3
Farragut North: Y1
Farragut West: B2, C6, D1, E2, F1, I1, I2, M4, O2, O5, R1, U3, W2, Y2
Federal Center SW: E1, H1, M5, N7, S4
Federal Triangle: C5, E5, J5, M2, N6, N8, P1, P2
Foggy Bottom: C4, H4, J3, K1, L4, N1, S1, S6, V3 [including
Georgetown: D3, F5, F7, O1, O4, U4]
L'Enfant Plaza: A1, E1, E4, H3, H6, N2, N5, O3, S5
McPherson Square: C7, L2, T2, U3, V1, W2, Y1
Metro Center: N8, P1, W2
Navy Yard—Ballpark: T1, X1
Pentagon: D2
Smithsonian: A1, B4, C6, D1, E4, F1, F6, H2, H6, I1, J2, J4, M1, N1, N2, N5, N6, O5, R1, S5, V3, W1, W3
Union Station: C2, H5, J1, L3, L5, S2, S3, S7, U1, U2
Waterfront: X1
Woodley Park—Zoo: C3, E3, G1, Q1, V2, Z1

Index of Major Prayer Topics

children and families: A3, E1, N5, N7, N9, Q1, S1, S5, T1, U2, V1, W2, Z1

confession and repentance: Preface, B3, B4, C2, M1, P1

*diplomacy and negotiations: Introduction, C1, C2, C4, C6, D3, E3, F7, L5, M4, O5, U3

*education and the arts: A2, B3, D3, E1, L3, M5, N1, N2, N4, N5, N6, N7, N8, Q1, S5, U4, Y1, Y2, Z1, Conclusion

*executive branch: Introduction, A1, B2, C4, C5, D2, E1, E2, E4, E5, F6, H1, H3, H6, I1, J2, J5, L1, L2, L4, M2, O2, O3, P2, S4, S6, T1, T2, U3, V1, V2, W1, W2, Conclusion

*financial and business sector: B4, F1, F2, I2, L1, S2, S4, U2, X1

freedom and human rights: A3, F5, F6, J1, J2, J3, J5, K1, L4, L5, M1, M3, N6, N7, O5, P1, Q1, S5, U1, U2, V2, W1

*healthcare and first responders: F3, H1, H4, L2, M2, R1, W3

*judicial branch: Introduction, C7, J5, M3, S7, Conclusion

*legislative branch: Introduction, C2, C4, H5, S3, Conclusion

*military: A3, D1, D2, F5, H2, J1, J3, J4, K1, M3, N9, P1, R1, V2, V3, W1, W3, Y1, Y2

*nature: A1, B1, B3, E4, E5, I1, N5, Z1, Conclusion

*spiritual life: C3, G1, H2, L4, M1, M5, N3, N6, O1, O4, Q1, S1, U1, U4, Y1, Y2

wisdom: Introduction, A1, C2, C5, C7, E1, E4, E5, G1, H1, H3, H6, I1, J2, L3, L4, N4, N5, N8, P1, Q1, S3, S5, S6, S7, T1, T2, V2, W2, X1, Z1, Conclusion

*Reader's Tip: Praying through each of the ten starred topics will cover the entire itinerary at least once.

Endnotes

[1] www.nps.gov/paav/index.htm, accessed September 2020.

[2] Every street has NW, NE, SE, or SW designations, some of which have been streamlined here to reduce repetition.

[3] This house is the only eighteenth-century building connected to the founding of D.C.; historicsites.dcpreservation.org/items/show/206, accessed September 2020.

[4] William Tindall, *Standard History of the City of Washington* (Knoxville: H.W. Crew & Co., 1914) 76; books.google.com/books?id=D_6ZDwAAQBAJ&pg=PT80&lpg=PT80&dq=Suter%27s+Tavern+on+March+29th+1791--George+Washington%27s+Diary&source=bl&ots=BGe40rD2Vq&sig=ACfU3U0eMZhMh7ewikc652nc8gNXAqoIXA&hl=en&sa=X&ved=2ahUKEwiD_I-fj7TpAhVKXc0KHZLECg4Q6AEwBXoECAcQAQ#v=onepage&q=Suter's%20Tavern%20on%20March%2029th%201791--George%20Washington's%20Diary&f=false, accessed September 2020.

[5] historicsites.dcpreservation.org/items/show/206, accessed September 2020; tile.loc.gov/storage-services/master/pnp/habshaer/dc/dc0100/dc0112/data/dc0112data.pdf, accessed September 2020.

[6] www.thoughtco.com/washington-dc-geography-1435747, accessed September 2020.

[7] www.fas.usda.gov/about-fas, accessed September 2020.

[8] www.arlingtoncemetery.mil/Explore/Monuments-and-Memorials/President-John-F-Kennedy-Gravesite, accessed September 2020.

[9] www.aoc.gov/capitol-buildings/bartholdi-park-and-fountain, accessed September 2020.

[10] www.blairhouse.org/history/the-blairs, accessed September 2020.

[11] www.usbg.gov/brief-history-us-botanic-garden, accessed September 2020.

[12] www.sil.si.edu/DigitalCollections/usexex/learn/Philbrick.htm, accessed September 2020.

[13] www.nytimes.com/2003/11/30/books/the-ex-ex-files.html?mcubz=1, accessed September 2020.

[14] bep.gov/uscurrency/history.html, accessed September 2020.

[15] www.aoc.gov/capitol-grounds/about-grounds, accessed September 2020.

[16] billygraham.org/story/a-legacy-of-revival-in-the-nations-capital/, accessed September 2020.

[17] www.hymnal.net/en/hymn/h/1048, accessed September 2020.

[18] www.visitthecapitol.gov/about-capitol/evolution-capitol, accessed September 2020.

[19] Ibid.

[20] www.newadvent.org/cathen/10198d.htm, accessed September 2020.

[21] cathedral.org/history/timeline/, accessed September 2020.

[22] www.dni.gov/index.php/who-we-are/history, accessed September 2020.

[23] www.commerce.gov/about, accessed September 2020.

[24] www.worldatlas.com/articles/the-territories-of-the-united-states.html, accessed September 2020.

[25] www.nps.gov/coga/learn/historyculture/index.htm, accessed September 2020.

26 www.archives.gov/founding-docs/declaration-transcript, accessed September 2020.

27 www.dar.org/national-society/about-dar/dar-history, accessed September 2020.

28 www.defense.gov/About/, accessed September 2020.

29 www.doaks.org/about/history, accessed September 2020.

30 www2.ed.gov/about/landing.jhtml, accessed September 2020.

31 www.history.com/topics/us-presidents/dwight-d-eisenhower, accessed September 2020.

32 Although TSC does not usually archive complete services, the church regularly streams worship at: tsc.nyc/webcasts/sunday-nyc/, accessed August 2020.

33 techcrunch.com/2017/01/01/no-cobalt-no-tesla/, accessed September 2020.

34 www.federalreserve.gov/aboutthefed.htm, accessed September 2020.

35 www.ftc.gov/about-ftc/what-we-do, accessed September 2020.

36 www.ftc.gov/about-ftc/our-history, accessed September 2020.

37 www.nps.gov/fomc/learn/historyculture/francis-scott-key.htm, accessed September 2020.

38 www.smithsonianmag.com/history/the-story-behind-the-star-spangled-banner-149220970/, accessed September 2020.

39 amhistory.si.edu/starspangledbanner/pdf/ssb_lyrics.pdf, accessed September 2020.

40 www.nps.gov/frde/learn/photosmultimedia/quotations.htm, accessed September 2020.

41 www.history.com/this-day-in-history/franco-american-alliances-signed, accessed September 2020.

42 www.saintsophiadc.com/about/history/, accessed September 2020.

43 www.hhs.gov/about/strategic-plan/introduction/index.html, accessed September 2020.

44 www.law.cornell.edu/constitution/fourth_amendment, accessed September 2020.

45 portal.hud.gov/hudportal/HUD?src=/about/hud_history, accessed September 2020.

46 www.doi.gov/whoweare/history/, accessed September 2020.

47 www.osmre.gov/about.shtm, accessed September 2020.

48 www.imf.org/en/About, accessed September 2020.

49 www.njamemorial.org/forced-removal-and-incarceration, accessed September 2020; www.njamemorial.org/american-soldiers, accessed September 2020.

50 In the early 600s, the Pantheon was transformed from a pagan worship space into a church: Santa Maria ad Martyres. The Christian community in Rome helped protect and maintain this building from the early Middle Ages to the present; www.pantheonroma.com/pantheon-history/, accessed September 2020.

51 www.washingtonpost.com/news/answer-sheet/wp/2015/07/04/are-our-rights-inalienable-or-unalienable/, accessed September 2020.

52 www.nps.gov/thje/learn/historyculture/memorialfeatures.htm, accessed September 2020.

53 lemelson.mit.edu/resources/john-ericsson, accessed September 2020; www.nps.gov/nama/planyourvisit/john-ericsson-memorial.htm, accessed September 2020.

[54] www.ancient.eu/Tyre/, accessed September 2020.

[55] www.nps.gov/revwar/about_the_revolution/jp_jones.html, accessed September 2020.

[56] www.koreanwarvetsmemorial.org/the-memorial/, accessed September 2020.

[57] www.dol.gov/general/aboutdol/history/dolhistoxford, accessed September 2020.

[58] www.nps.gov/whho/planyourvisit/explore-the-northern-trail.htm#CP_JUMP_2801813, accessed September 2020.

[59] For legal definitions of modern slavery and an explanation of its extent, see the State Department's annual Trafficking in Persons Report: www.state.gov/wp-content/uploads/2020/06/2020-TIP-Report-Complete-062420-FINAL.pdf, accessed September 2020.

[60] www.loc.gov/about/history-of-the-library/, accessed September 2020.

[61] www.loc.gov/about/, accessed September 2020.

[62] www.folger.edu/history/founders, accessed September 2020.

[63] Daniel Swift, *Shakespeare's Common Prayers: The Book of Common Prayer and the Elizabethan Age* (New York: Oxford University Press, 2012) frontispiece and 37-38. Note also Bob Hostetler's 2016 article: www.guideposts.org/faith-and-prayer/prayer-stories/pray-effectively/7-ways-to-pray-with-shakespeare, accessed September 2020.

[64] Act IV, Scene 1, Lines 182-83, 185, 194-95, and 197-200; shakespeare.mit.edu/merchant/merchant.4.1.html, accessed September 2020.

[65] www.nps.gov/linc/learn/historyculture/memorial-features.htm, accessed September 2020.

[66] www.nps.gov/linc/learn/historyculture/inscriptions.htm, accessed September 2020.

[67] www.archives.gov/exhibits/featured-documents/emancipation-proclamation/transcript.html, accessed September 2020.

[68] crdl.usg.edu/events/prayer_pilgrimage/?Welcome, accessed September 2020.

[69] www.nps.gov/mlkm/learn/building-the-memorial.htm, accessed September 2020.

[70] www.nps.gov/mlkm/learn/quotations.htm, accessed September 2020.

[71] See p. 11 at okra.stanford.edu/transcription/document_images/undecided/630416-019.pdf, accessed September 2020.

[72] dmv.dc.gov/node/1118901, accessed September 2020.

[73] www.loc.gov/law/help/statutes-at-large/29th-congress/session-1/c29s1ch35.pdf, accessed September 2020.

[74] constitutioncenter.org/interactive-constitution/amendments/amendment-xxiii, accessed September 2020.

[75] americanart.si.edu/collections/search/artwork/?id=9445, accessed September 2020.

[76] intowner.com/2013/01/13/the-seven-buildings-some-of-washingtons-earliest-townhouses-now-a-building-billboard/, accessed September 2020.

[77] christiannews.net/2020/07/24/2020-state-of-the-bible-report-finds-few-americans-read-bible-daily/, accessed September 2020.

[78] www.nationalacademies.org/about, accessed September 2020.

[79] airandspace.si.edu/history-0, accessed September 2020.

[80] ncnw.org/ncnw/our-history, accessed September 2020; www.nps.gov/mamc/planyourvisit/upload/Bethune-Trail.pdf, accessed September 2020.

[81] www.nps.gov/people/dorothy-i-height.htm, accessed September 2020.

[82] kinginstitute.stanford.edu/king-papers/documents/i-have-dream-address-delivered-march-washington-jobs-and-freedom, accessed September 2020.

[83] mellon.org/about/history/andrew-w-mellon/, accessed September 2020.

[84] nmaahc.si.edu/about/museum, accessed September 2020.

[85] thenationaldc.org/history/, accessed September 2020.

[86] www.navymemorial.org/commemorative-plaque-program, accessed September 2020.

[87] www.nga.gov/press/2014/collaboration.html, accessed September 2020.

[88] https://www.oakhillcemeterydc.org/visit/map, accessed September 2020; georgetownmetropolitan.com/2010/03/18/the-famous-tenants-of-oak-hill-cemetery/, accessed September 2020.

[89] www.acf.hhs.gov/orr, accessed September 2020.

[90] www.tourofdc.org/tours/OldStoneHouse/, accessed September 2020.

[91] www.oas.org/en/about/our_history.asp, accessed September 2020.

[92] museum.oas.org/about.html, accessed September 2020.

[93] www.nps.gov/articles/pershing-park.htm, accessed September 2020.

[94] www.history.com/this-day-in-history/u-s-postal-system-established, accessed September 2020.

[95] Frame of Government of Pennsylvania, 1682; avalon.law.yale.edu/17th_century/pa04.asp#:~:text=The%20Preface,integrity%20to%20use%20them%20justly, accessed September 2020.

[96] www.redcross.org/about-us/who-we-are/history, accessed September 2020.

[97] salvationarmynca.org/about-us/history/, accessed September 2020; www.salvationarmyusa.org/usn/history-of-the-salvation-army/, accessed September 2020.

[98] www.sechistorical.org/museum/about/, accessed September 2020.

[99] www.si.edu/museums/arts-and-industries-building, accessed September 2020.

[100] siarchives.si.edu/history/smithsonian-institution-building-castle, accessed September 2020.

[101] siarchives.si.edu/history/james-smithson, accessed September 2020.

[102] siarchives.si.edu/history/national-zoological-park, accessed September 2020.

[103] hirshhorn.si.edu/explore/the-founding-donor/, accessed September 2020.

[104] www.pbs.org/becomingamerican/ap_pjourneys_transcript5e.html, accessed September 2020.

[105] www.state.gov/about/about-the-u-s-department-of-state/, accessed September 2020.

[106] www.britannica.com/place/Washington-DC/History, accessed September 2020.

[107] www.bluffton.edu/homepages/facstaff/sullivanm/washdc/unionsta/unionstation.html, accessed September 2020.

[108] www.christianitytoday.com/history/issues/issue-28/313-edict-of-milan.html, accessed September 2020.

[109] teamster.org/about/frequently-asked-questions-faq/, accessed September 2020.

110 www.va.gov/about_va/programs.asp, accessed September 2020.

111 www.usno.navy.mil/USNO/about-us/a-brief-history, accessed September 2020.

112 www.nps.gov/vive/learn/collections.htm, accessed September 2020.

113 www.nps.gov/wamo/learn/historyculture/index.htm, accessed September 2020.

114 www.nps.gov/wamo/index.htm, accessed September 2020.

115 www.nps.gov/wamo/learn/historyculture/earthquake.htm, accessed September 2020.

116 www.pbs.org/wgbh/nova/egypt/raising/luxor.html, accessed September 2020.

117 www.visitthecapitol.gov/about-capitol/evolution-capitol, accessed September 2020.

118 www.nps.gov/flni/index.htm, accessed September 2020.

119 www.theguardian.com/world/2001/dec/02/september11.terrorism1, accessed September 2020.

120 www.nps.gov/whho/planyourvisit/explore-the-northern-trail.htm#CP_JUMP_2801813, accessed September 2020.

121 www.nps.gov/wwii/learn/historyculture/index.htm, accessed September 2020.

122 www.history.com/topics/world-war-ii/tuskegee-airmen, accessed September 2020.

123 www.si.com/xfl/2020/04/13/xfl-bankruptcy, accessed September 2020.

124 www.ymca.int/member/ymca-in-europe/ymca-england-wales/, accessed September 2020.

125 www.asymca.org/history, accessed September 2020.

126 nationalzoo.si.edu/animals/exhibits, accessed September 2020.

127 www.cdc.gov/plague/index.html, accessed September 2020.

128 americanhistory.si.edu/presidency/1b2.html, accessed September 2020.

129 www.jfklibrary.org/Research/Research-Aids/Ready-Reference/JFK-Quotations/Inaugural-Address.aspx, accessed September 2020.

Made in the USA
Monee, IL
26 September 2020